Hi Adrienne,

Thanks you
from all of us
at r logical for your
faith and support
throughout the
years!

With gratitude,
Joe

SWAGGER

The "Way of the Sway" to Sales and Life Success

Joseph Gianni

2logical Publishing, Inc.

Published by:

2logical Publishing, Inc.
500 Linden Oaks, Rochester, NY 14625

Visit our website at www.2logical.com

Printed in the United States of America

First Edition
Hardcover ISBN: 978-0-692-82382-8

Contents

Introduction: BORN TO SWAGGER   7

Part I: THE RESULTS OF A SALES CAREER AND LIFE BUILT TO SWAGGER   17

1   Everyone Wants to Swagger   19

Part II: SWAGGER SELLING: AN IDEA WHOSE TIME HAS COME   27

2   Transforming an Idea into Reality   29
3   Sales is a Contact Sport —And So is Building a Life With Swagger   35
4   Swagger-Set: A Mindset Comprised of Optimal Beliefs   45
5   Unlocking Your Swagger: Is There a Master Key?   49
6   Swagger-Set: A Mind Matrix Comprised of Five Core Beliefs   53

Part III: The MASTER OF FUNDAMENTAL SELLING SKILLS: THE CALLING CARD OF ALL THOSE WHO SELL WITH SWAGGER   69

7   The Master of Fundamental Sales Skills   71
8   The Secret to Establishing Rapport   83
9   The Power of a Well Organized and Executed Transitional Success Story   95

10 The Key to Consultative Selling: Becoming a Master
   Qualifier   **105**

11 Creating a Strategic Sales Presentation   **129**

12 Closing Your Way To the Top—The Place Where All
   Those With Swagger Sit   **149**

13 Overcoming Sales Objections/Resistance   **165**

14 Prospecting: The Prelude to Sales Success   **185**

Epilogue   **213**
The Reason Why

Appendix A
Swagger Stories   **219**

Appendix B
Recommended Resources   **249**

Appendix C
Can Swagger Be Implemented at an Enterprise Level?   **253**

Appendix D
Acknowledgments   **259**

SWAGGER

*The "Way of the Sway" to
Sales and Life Success*

Introduction:

BORN TO SWAGGER

Introduction

BORN TO SWAGGER

Let the Journey Begin!

An hour after I received my college diploma on a hot and humid day, I kissed and hugged my mom and dad goodbye for now and leaped into my car with all of my worldly possessions in the trunk and my fiancée, Michelle, by my side. I remember this day vividly, for it was the day I mentally cut the umbilical cord and ventured on to do what my parents raised me to do: chase my dreams!

With nothing more than a few hundred dollars in my checking account, I moved to Webster, New York, a little suburb just a few miles east of the city of Rochester—home at the time to industry leaders like Eastman Kodak, Xerox, and Bausch & Lomb. My dream was to someday be an entrepreneur, just like the founders of these iconic companies, but by doing what? I had no idea.

I did know one thing, however: Whatever business I would one day start, I would need to be able to **sell**. Otherwise I would most likely never succeed.

I began my employment search, but unlike most college graduates, I had zero interest in obtaining a job. Instead, I knew I needed to find a mentor. I wanted to find a leader who could and would teach me sales skills and abilities at an extreme level.

It was 1982, and a recession gripped the country, so the pickings were slim in the job market. I went on countless interviews looking for a mentor, but I could not find one. Interview after interview, I prepared by reading about the company and the industry; however, when I met the various sales managers and executives, I found they were not particularly prepared considering their profession—and, more importantly, not particularly accomplished. I was offered positions, but I did not want to work for people who were just mediocre at what they did. I wanted to find and work for the best!

Then one day, I answered an ad placed by Macmillan Publishing Company. I passed the pre-screening phone interview and secured a face-to-face meeting with the regional sales manager.

As I knocked on the door, I heard a man's deep voice bellow, "Just one moment." I rolled my eyes as I thought about how this buffoon, who kept me waiting in the lobby for more than an hour past my scheduled interview time, was going to be just another big waste of my time...but then the door swung open with the force of a watershed that had given way.

Standing in the doorway was a towering man, about six-foot-three, who extended his hand for a shake and said, "Hi, I'm Randy. Pleased to meet you."

Hesitantly, I extended my hand in return, and as our hands clasped he looked right into my eyes with a fire and warmth I had never quite experienced before.

Despite this forceful introduction, however, I was unfazed—I was still a little perturbed that he kept me waiting so long. Randy turned and said, "Please come in and have a seat. I am particularly sorry to have kept you waiting. I'm interviewing eighty people over three days for this open sales position and I have to admit, I am running a little bit behind."

Behind, my ass, I thought. Still, I could not help but notice how poised, polite and professional this man was, now that we finally met.

As he commenced the interview, in what was by far the most organized and professional manner I had ever seen during my weeks of searching, he explained how the interview process would be conducted. He would ask me a series of questions to learn about my background and to learn about "me" as an individual. He went on to say that after he was done, he would give me an opportunity to ask any questions I might have for him.

Upon completing one of the most engaging and insightful interviews I had ever had, he said, "Joe, do you have any questions for me?"

"Yes," I said, "I have just a few."

"Okay," he said, "Please ask away."

"Well, Randy, can you tell me how your sales team performed last year?"

"Quite well," he replied.

"How well?" I said, "If you don't mind me asking."

He chuckled a little and said, "We were number one."

I immediately straightened up further in my chair and said slowly, "R-e-a-l-l-y," followed by, "Why are you chuckling?"

He calmly stopped smiling, sat forward and said, "Joe, you do not understand. You see, we are number one every year."

"You are?" I said.

"Yes."

"Tell me, how do you do this?"

"It's quite simple," he replied. "I train my people."

At that instant I knew I had finally found what I was looking for.

When you knock with a singleness of purpose, the door to Swagger Selling will open.

Luck, fate, preparation I will let you decide, but I was blessed that day when he offered me an opportunity to join his team on the spot. (I do still wonder to this very moment what he did with the other ten people who were waiting for him in the lobby). I accepted, and soon found myself on a plane flying to New York City for orientation.

At the Macmillan corporate office, I had a walk-through tour of the company. As we turned each corner, the administrative assistant introduced me to the various marketing managers and editors by saying, "This is Mark, he is marketing manager, and he used to work for Randy...and this is Bill, an editor for our business books, and he used to work for Randy." This continued as we made our way throughout the office, concluding with, "And you see this editor coming up the hall, she used to work for..."

I stopped her before she could finish, "I'm guessing, Randy."

"Yes," she smiled and walked me to the training room, where Randy greeted me, and I learned that besides being a regional sales manager, he had a second title—Director of Sales Training.

Like a bucking thoroughbred thrashing at the gate, when I finally landed back in Rochester, I stepped off of the plane and my career exploded…just like the careers of everyone else who joined this special leader's team. I quickly became a top producer in the company. By the end of my second year, I was promoted to District Sales Manager, followed by three other promotions to Regional Sales Manager, National Sales Trainer and Director of Marketing. This last promotion I turned down, because I knew I was ready to start my own company.

As I reflect, I would love to say that my sales results and career success up to that point came to pass because I was so darn talented that day I joined the company. The catalyst for my success, however— and the extraordinary success of my peers on the mid-Atlantic regional sales team— was that we were trained; but not trained simply with the traditional ways and methodologies of selling "skills" and "process" …we were trained to **Swagger**, even though up to that very moment in time, I did not realize it just yet.

An Unexpected Phone Call

When the phone rang one morning, I could tell by the stillness on the line that something was amiss.

"Joe, this is Randy. Do you have a moment?"

"Sure."

"I need to tell you something."

"Okay, what's up?"

He explained that he was leaving Macmillan. He was well known within the industry, and he received "an offer he just couldn't refuse" from a much larger publishing company.

"Joe, I want you to come with me," he said next, "and if you do, I will give you half of the national sales force to run in the first year; and I will give you the entire country to run starting your second year. And I give you my word!"

If he gave me his word, I knew I could bank on it. At the ripe age of twenty-five, I knew this was an extraordinary offer…but as tempting as it was, I knew I didn't want to do it. "Randy," I said, "I am overwhelmed and flattered by your offer, but as you know, my dream" —and he surely did know because as a leader of people, he took the time to know— "is to be an entrepreneur."

At that moment in time, that's as much as I could say. An entrepreneur doing what? I had no idea!

Without skipping a beat, Randy chuckled and said, "I know, my friend, but I had to ask."

As we concluded the call, I said that I needed to take him to lunch or dinner before he departed, to thank him for all that he had done for me.

In preparation for our lunch, I bought a blank thank you card the prior day. I wanted to take the time to write this man, my mentor, a letter to thank him for all that he had selflessly given to me.

As I sat at my kitchen table, I pondered what I could say that would embody the magnitude of what he had done for me. I mentally began to write my words of thanks:

Dear Randy,

Thank you for teaching me professional selling to such an extreme level that I know I will one day become financially independent because of the refined selling skills you have bequeathed to me.

As I sat and wrote this in my mind, however, I realized it was so much more. In my second mental attempt, I wrote:

Dear Randy,

Thanks for teaching me leadership and management to such a refined level—how to recruit, train and motivate others—that I know I am destined for major career success in this vocation...

But still, it was so much more than that. I realized that because of what this man had taught me, I was a better child to my parents, a better sibling to my brothers, a better friend to my friends, a better spouse to my wife. I was never bad at any of these roles, but I realized that because of what this man taught me, I was just better in every aspect of my life. Heck, as I sat swimming in my thoughts, I realized this, too: I knew I would even be a better father to my children, even though I didn't have children yet.

Finally, I could write my thank you letter.

The next day I jumped into the car and headed to Downingtown, Pennsylvania, to have lunch with my friend. As you can imagine, our lunch was filled with reminiscences of all the hard work but also the tremendous fun we had shared. We laughed hard for several hours. It was truly bittersweet. As we concluded our time together, I turned to Randy and said in a solemn tone, "I really can't thank you or ever repay you for what you have done for me and given to me. However, I did try as best I could to capture it in this letter I wrote you last night."

My intention was that Randy would take the letter and read it later that evening...but instead, he asked what I was quietly hoping I could avoid ..."Joe, if you do not mind, I would like to read it now. Is that okay?"

Hesitantly and with great trepidation, I said, "Okay."

Within moments he pulled the card from the envelope and read these words:

Dear Randy,
    Thanks for taking the time to teach me how to sell and live life with Swagger!
My love and respect,
Joe

You see, what Randy taught me, and what he taught every salesperson that ever crossed his path, was how to Swagger: a mental dance that starts and ends with the understanding that *the greatest sale we will ever learn to make, is the sale we make to ourselves first, to be the best we can be at whatever role we assume in life.*

My friend, my mentor, did not simply tell people this. He was a master of helping people actually learn how to do it...a magical and rhythmical journey I had experienced and of which I was a major beneficiary.

In short, Randy taught his people—including me—how to live, love and sell with Swagger. And little did I realize that at that very moment, he was about to plant a career-altering seed in my mind as we parted ways, by asking me one final question.

"Joe, in all the years we have known each other, I have never asked for anything. But today I would like to ask you for a personal favor. Will you help me?"

"Sure, Randy," I quickly replied. "What do you need?"

He smiled ever so slightly—just like he did the very first day we met—but did not reply. I can still see that face he always made, every time he was about to twist my mind. Nervously, I broke the silence and asked, "Do you need money?"

He quickly chuckled and said, "Hell, no, I do not need your money. I have plenty of money."

Thank God, I thought, because I had been saving money like a chipmunk saves nuts for the winter since I was ten years old—the seed capital I knew I would need to start my own business. But if that man had asked me for my life's savings, I would have given it to him without hesitation. Why? Because he had earned it all and then some for what he had given me.

"Randy," I slowly said, "Do you need help moving?"

He titled his head, much like a young puppy does when it hears a sound that it completely cannot fathom. "Absolutely not. The new company will move me."

I again thought *Thank God,* because he was moving from Downingtown, Pennsylvania, to San Francisco, and that would have been a nightmare.

Again I looked at Randy and that ever so slight smile on his face, and asked anxiously, "Randy, what do you need?"

His smile faded, and with a look and a measured voice that you might imagine a prophet would use, he said, "I want you to go find your Joe Gianni, and take the time to teach him or her what I have taken the time to teach you. Will you do that for me?"

As if I had heard a strange new noise, I angled my head in thought, straightened it back up, looked him in the eyes and said, "You have my word!"

A few short years later, I finally started my company: a global sales and leadership training company that has taught individuals just like you around the world how to live, love and sell your way through life with Swagger.

Are you ready to see and learn how to Swagger, too?

If so, let's turn the page and start swaying to the beat of all those who know how to Swagger!

Part I:

THE RESULTS OF A SALES CAREER AND LIFE BUILT TO SWAGGER

Chapter 1:

EVERYONE WANTS TO SWAGGER

With 19 seconds left on the clock and the score was Utah 86, Chicago 85, Michael Jordan didn't stand around questioning his ability to intercept the ball, drive it down the court and make the winning shot. He kept his eye on the ball, easily grabbed it from the Jazz player and in a few strides, crossed over his defender and sank a jumper for the win.

When Joe Montana trailed the Cincinnati Bengals in Super Bowl XXIII with just 3:10 left on the clock, he didn't stop to doubt whether he could lead the San Francisco 49ers to victory. He started throwing one pass after another, grabbing first downs until the 49ers scored the winning touchdown in one of the biggest drives in NFL's history: 92 yards in 11 plays. I was in the stands that day, and watched Montana and his team rip the win out of the grasp of the Bengals and leave the stadium with the victory.

When Steve Jobs returned to Apple after leaving in disgrace a few years before, he didn't sit around nursing feelings of inadequacy and self-doubt. He got to work with his creative team and produced the iMac, introducing the candy-colored computers to a huge rally of loyal fans and placing Apple back in competition for the top computing company in the world.

When 26-year-old Audra MacDonald took the Broadway stage in her first major role as Carrie Pipperidge in *Carousel*, she did not let the fact that she was the first black woman in history to play the role "slow her roll." Not only did she play Carrie with grace and musical skill, but she won the Tony Award for her efforts—the first of three Tonys she would collect in a scant five years.

When Leonardo DiCaprio was passed over for the Oscar for his performances in *The Aviator* and *The Wolf of Wall Street*, he did not give up on Hollywood or start giving lackluster performances. Instead, he took on the role of Hugh Glass in *The Revenant*, one of the most challenging and complex roles of his career—for which he finally won the Oscar.

In 1940 and 1941, when Nazi forces rained bombs down on 16 cities in England, Prime Minister Winston Churchill did not allow himself to become demoralized by the destruction. Even when London became the enemy's prime target for 57 consecutive nights in September and October 1940, he maintained British production of weapons, kept the economy on track, and led the defense of England with skill and courage.

And when Martin Luther King, Jr., led more than 25,000 people on a march from Selma to Montgomery, Alabama in 1963 to protest discriminatory voting rights laws, he did not hesitate to stand on the steps of the state capitol to speak even when the threat of personal harm and violence was a clear and present danger.

It is not difficult to see that these icons from across vocations dance through life to a different beat…they move with Swagger! We can all see it, and we can all recognize it as we observe their massive life accomplishments:

- Michael Jordan became the single greatest NBA player of all time.
- Joe Montana was named Most Valuable Player twice by the Associated Press, was elected to eight Pro Bowls, and had the highest passer rating in the NFL in 1987 and 1989. In 2000, he was inducted into the Pro Football Hall of Fame.
- Steve Jobs led Apple to become the largest and most successful company in the world.
- Audra McDonald is a six-time Tony Award winner who can choose any role on stage or screen.
- Leo DiCaprio is heralded as one of the greatest actors of our time.
- Winston Churchill led England to victory in World War II.
- Martin Luther King, Jr. played a critical role in passage of the Civil Rights Act in 1964 and led a movement that changed the course of history.

There is no denying the results of those who walk amongst us with Swagger.

But can we define it? Can it be taught?

Can everyone learn how to Swagger?

Swagger Defined

The simple truth is that everyone can walk life's road, professionally and personally, with Swagger. Each of us can build a life fueled by dreams and the progressive realization of those dreams. However, to do so, we must understand the origin and ingredients to those that master the "way of the sway."

What is Swagger?

Merriam-Webster's Dictionary defines swagger as 1. To walk in a very confident way, to walk with swagger. 2. A way of walking or behaving that shows you have a lot of confidence. 3. Marked by elegance or showiness.

However, to some, the word Swagger can be defined with a negative connotation of cockiness, arrogance, or ostentatious display of bravado. Nevertheless, there is no denying that the **results** of those with Swagger are demonstrably greater than those who lack the ability to strut through life with Swagger.

I personally think the best definition of Swagger is found in the Urban Dictionary. It describes those with Swagger this way: "How one presents him or herself to the world. Swagger is shown from how a person handles a situation."

To me, and to today's millennial generation, this defines those with Swagger best because it is simple, vivid and results-based… meaning those with Swagger get bigger, better, stronger results in all of life's endeavors. But why? Because of the way they act and react to life situations.

How?

That, my friends, is the essence of what this book is about, and it is exactly what my friend and mentor, Randy, taught me at the age of 21.

Simply explained, people that exude Swagger in all that they dream, attempt and ultimately do in life do not have the same thoughts and beliefs about themselves, others, or their propensity to achieve results in life.

People with Swagger have a different mindset. I call it a Swagger-Set, a set of core governing beliefs from which they operate. As such, the way they act, react and interface with others and the world as a whole is different from the overwhelming majority of people in equal or similar roles in life.

Whether it is a career role in sales, leadership and management, operations, customer service, or a life role as a parent, friend, coach, teacher...those who learn to walk with Swagger in each respective role dramatically outperform those who never learn how.

The Road Less Traveled

Whether your vocation is in sports, the arts, public service, or professional sales, it is a well-known fact that the road less traveled is the one defined by those who become the best that they can be—versus opting out for a life defined by mediocrity and often less than average performance. I do not state this observation with a judge's robe on, and the fact is I have met some people who truly are content to take life as it simply comes to them.

However, I have met far more people who *want* to live a world of career and life abundance, but truly do not know where or how to begin to build it.

As a sales trainer and the CEO and President of an internationally well-known and recognized workforce development company, I can assure you that most business leaders and people as a whole want to compete in their career and the game of life to win—and to win big!

Yet they are imprisoned in a collective mindset by a world that breeds mediocrity. Again, I do not state this fact in a judgmental or preaching kind of way. I simply state it as an observation I have made through the mental prism I adopted when I learned to Swagger as a young man and professional in sales.

The Greatest Sale You Will Ever Learn to Make...

The greatest sale you will ever learn to make is the one you make to yourself first—to be the best you can be at whatever role you commit to in life.

These are the words that succinctly summarize and illuminate the journey you must take if you wish to learn how to live life with Swagger!

These 32 words embody the core philosophy of those who seek to Swagger Sell in their career and in life. They are easy words to say, yet difficult to embrace—because few are helped to see exactly how to subscribe to a life of Swagger.

Henry David Thoreau said it best: "The mass of men live lives of quiet desperation, and go to the grave with the song still in them."

This simple statement by Thoreau back in 1854 still bears truth for far too many of those we all know today.

We do not need to search long and hard to bear witness to the mediocrity we see that has become the norm in countless pockets of society's great institutions: It permeates our K-12 education system, it exists throughout our local, state and federal government, and it is easily observable in the deterioration of the family structure and unit.

I share this not to depress you and me. I share this to help crystallize the fact that building your sales career and life with Swagger is truly the road less traveled.

Jack-of-All-Trades, Master of None

Most people in professional sales become the Jack-Of-All-Trades, and the master of none.

What I mean is simply this: The overwhelming amount of people in professional sales invest 30-plus years in this awesome career, and yet never master the fundamental selling skills and process that will make them great!

Why?

To bring our discussion back to center stage—meaning you and your sales career—the point I am making is that mediocrity is prevalent and commonplace throughout our society. You have no doubt witnessed this, and by default perhaps have lived it yourself to date in your sales career.

Most people never master the core fundamentals of how to consistently prospect (capture referrals, develop centers of influences), and they never become lethal at executing each stage of the sales process:

- Build **rapport**
- Perfect the transition from rapport to the qualify, through mastery of a **Transitional Success Story**
- **Qualify**—logically and emotionally
- Perfect a **presentation** that dances from start to finish
- **Close** and consistently **convert objections into deals**

It is not hard to imagine an individual in your and my vocation of professional sales that has 10, 20, 30-plus years of experience, but can't close…or does not consistently referral-prospect or qualify. It is not hard to imagine, because as a consultant, I see it everywhere I go, and you do, too. In fact, what I am describing may very well be what you personify to date in your sales career. And you know what? I am here to tell you: It does not matter!

What I mean is this: It is not good, it is not bad; it simply is. All that matters is what *you* do about it. It is never too early and never too late to begin your journey to professional and personal excellence. It is never too early or too late to get your Swagger on!

The Price of Mediocrity

Is there a price to pay for settling for mediocrity in sales and in life? You bet there is.

But is there a price to pay for learning to swagger your way through life? You bet there is!

However, I want to assure you that price in terms of energy, effort, time, and financial resources is almost the same, meaning this: It takes just as much time, energy, effort and concentration to build and live a life of mediocrity, because of the opportunity cost debited daily to our life performance, or lack thereof, by not becoming the best. But besides the opportunity cost, let's face it: It takes just as much energy and effort to make up excuses for underperformance, and for the energy to hide and not apply ourselves, as it does to simply commit and apply oneself to becoming the best you can be.

Here's the bottom line: Although the costs in terms of effort and emotion are similar, the results in terms of respect, opportunity, satisfaction and financial gain for those who learn to Swagger are profoundly different from the results for those who do not!

So do you want to learn how to Swagger? Do you want to learn and master the "way of the sway?" If so, I implore you to read on. You will not be disappointed.

Part II:

Swagger Selling:
An Idea Whose Time Has Come

Chapter 2:

TRANSFORMING AN IDEA INTO REALITY

It was approximately twelve months after my luncheon with Randy... and what would come to be his prophetic statement regarding my career and life passion neatly camouflaged in his question: "Will you help me?"

I had made the commitment to find my own Joe Gianni and teach him or her all I had learned. But how would I do this?

And then, it finally hit me like a two-by-four right in the face at a construction site. I knew what business I was going to start.

No, I did not name it, "The Swagger Company." But it was exactly what this new company was going to bring to the corporate world. We were going to teach their salespeople and teams how to Swagger.

Heck, I had seen firsthand the results of a career, of a team and of lives transformed by learning how to Swagger. I sat back and pondered the idea: *I wonder if I could really start a business teaching those in sales how to Swagger.*

Armed with this unique vision and a daunting mission, I set out to discover exactly what the corporate world was doing to develop their most valuable asset: their people.

I quickly organized a meeting: a focus group, if you will, of sales executives, directors of training, and managers from across industry. I wanted to talk to these leaders about the type and content of training they utilized to develop their salespeople.

The focus group meeting commenced with an interactive chat about sales training and workforce development as a whole. About 15 to 20 minutes into the conversation, an amazing shift in the discussion occurred when one of the most senior level folks, the director of sales training at a Fortune 100 company, made the following statement:

"You know, we spend literally millions of dollars each year on employee development, and if I'm going to be completely candid today, I've got to share with you that so often much of the training we do doesn't work."

This, as you could imagine, was quite a profound statement that took place just 20 minutes into the discussion. So I asked, "What exactly do you mean by this?"

He looked directly and intently at each of us, and rapidly responded: "Well you know, what it really comes down to is this—when we do our training we find that no matter what the training is, whether it's sales training, management/leadership training, coaching and mentoring training, customer service training, process training, whatever training we do—**only about 5 percent** of the people who attend truly embrace the ideas and strategies, and go back to their work role and actually make true adjustments in behavior and thereby deliver bigger and better results—the results that we're after."

He went on, "Maybe about **another 15 or 20 percent** of them go back and might change one thing or embrace one new idea, but there are no real sweeping changes, no real adoption of new skills or changes in behaviors. The **remaining maybe 75 or 80 percent** do not demonstrate any change at all. Maybe there is a little spike in their morale because they are taken out of the day-to-day grind of their jobs, but there's no change whatsoever in their behaviors or the way they were doing things; no new skill or strategy adoption."

Bewildered, I looked around the room at the other leaders sitting at the table, and much to my surprise, they were all nodding their heads in agreement. So I simply asked that same executive, "Can you tell us what, exactly, do your best people look like?" Of course, I didn't mean in a physical or gender sense; I wanted him to share specifically what made these five percent of his people different.

He paused for a moment, and then confidently responded: "Well you know, they have initiative, they're self-motivated, they're extremely confident, they have strong self-esteem, they have a strong sense of self-efficacy, they're predominately positive in nature rather than negative, they're persistent, they're not victims of change, they're agents of change, they are able to handle setbacks and challenges and obstacles and consistently persevere."

As we looked around at the other leaders in the room, they all started nodding their heads again and they began to chime in, throwing out more descriptions: "They're extremely goal-directed, they're people that are committed and resilient."

It was an amazing moment, because everybody completely agreed that these are the attributes/abilities consistently observed in their top five percent.

As we completed this part of the discussion there was a long pause, and then I asked the group, "Well, if this is your unanimous description, the configuration of what your best people look like, what exactly do you do each year to develop them at this level? What type of training are you doing to teach them these core things, the things that you very carefully, and very quickly delineated as the most important difference of your best people; that five percent, the real movers and shakers in your organization?"

With a totally stunned look, like a deer in headlights, one of the other leaders in the room kind of stumbled a little bit and said, "Um, uh, um, not much," and the senior leader at the largest company represented—the one who had talked about his best people—literally leaned forward and chimed:

"We don't do anything at all at that level!"

Right then, right there, it was crystal clear to me: that in the corporate world, as dedicated as it has always been to helping and equipping the workforce with what they need to succeed, there remained a massive void! They did not recognize, nor did they understand the need to teach their people to Swagger.

This was a gap of monumental proportion that remains to this day the impetus of our company's mission: Help the corporate world develop peak performing sales professionals and work teams by implementing development at this core level first, the Mindset Level (the collection of optimal beliefs) which define all peak performing salespeople, the very same thoughts and beliefs that are embodied in all those who live, love and sell through life with Swagger.

The Swagger Success Model

On that very day, fueled by the insights and inspiration from our executive panel, we crystallized a simple yet powerful way to succinctly describe exactly how we could help our corporate clients teach their sales teams and workforce how to succeed—by instituting Swagger training on an enterprise level.

We call it **The Swagger Success Model,** and it looks like this:

As you can see, it's simple, succinct, and it is omnipotent when it comes to teaching you, me, and others how to get results—big results! The kind of results captured by those with Swagger!

Let me explain the power of these three words that comprise your path to mastery of Swagger Selling.

The first word is **Results**, because—to be candid—that is what we each are after (and so is your manager, as well as the company you work for). Results, or lack thereof, are how we all define success.

Results = Success

The second word is **Actions**. All of our Results each day, week, month and year are determined by our Actions. Simply put—in sales as in life—if we take the right Actions, we get the right Results. If we take the wrong Actions, we get the wrong Results. And as we all know and have seen, if we take a mishmash of actions—sometimes the right ones, and sometimes the wrong ones—the sum product is always mediocre results. (Unfortunately, this is how most people stumble through their sales careers and their lives.)

It is at the Actions level that 90 percent of most sales training (and any other training) takes place. This is the how-to level, the level where selling skills, sales process, and best practices are taught. It looks like this:

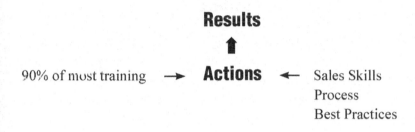

It's important to note that this level of career development for you, me and everyone is essential—in fact, *critical* to our success. However, you and I both know that just because someone shows us what and how to do something, it does not mean we will actually embrace it and practice it tirelessly until we master it.

We may both know this, but doing it is another story. Michael Jordan, with mere seconds on the clock, did not steal the ball and sink the shot devoid of skill any more than you or I are going to book a sales call and close a deal without knowing how, and without mastery of the sales skills needed to win when it matters the most!

This is where and why the third simple word of the Swagger Success Model comes to life and meaning:

Belief

You see, people do not act on new ideas, master new skills, execute on a new strategy or plan, until they first believe they are capable and worthy of doing so.

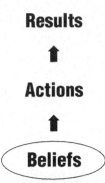

Results

⬆

Actions

⬆

Beliefs

Swagger stems from the belief level of personal and career development. People master the critical skills needed to execute the strategies/plans essential to their success because they have developed a set of core optimal beliefs about themselves, their self-efficacy, and the gift of life we have each been given.

It is with this specific tapestry of core beliefs—beliefs I have invested 30 years identifying and studying—from which all those who develop extreme skills produce the drive, ambition and conviction needed for talent mastery. Some may call these core beliefs a mindset—and they would be correct—but I prefer to affectionately call them the **Swagger-Set**.

As you read and digest the Swagger Success Model above, I want to urge you to read on to the next page. It is where I will reveal to you how I first witnessed the power and truth of what I described above. A truth I can now summarize in one simple statement:

All skills, talent and abilities are first born in the seed of a burning desire, fueled by a set of core beliefs, cradled in faith.

Chapter 3:

SALES IS A CONTACT SPORT— AND SO IS BUILDING A LIFE WITH SWAGGER

It was finally summer and I was excited to start the festivities of non-stop play with my childhood best friends, JoJo, Eddie and Norman. I was twelve years old at the time, but I remember it as vividly as if it were yesterday.

"Twenty-nine blue, hut, hut, hut, hike…" The ball was snapped, it was a warm Saturday morning and my friend Norman dropped back to throw the big pass. It was a little bit of a floater; just a little outside of the reach of my other friend Eddie, who dove for the pass and made the catch for another touchdown. Norm, as I always liked to call him, purposely floated the ball out in front of Eddie, knowing he would run past the defender and make the catch. Norm was a smart budding quarterback (in his mind), and our friend Eddie was crazy enough to dive for the ball, because we were playing on the street…a little tiny cul-de-sac off of Fawn Drive in East Islip, New York, where I grew up.

As Eddie was picking the pebbles out of his knees and elbow, I noticed Norman's dad ("Mr. E," as we affectionately called him), a man of towering physical stature, was standing on the edge of his driveway with a big smile, looking on at us. Without any hesitation, Norm turned to his dad and with unbridled enthusiasm shouted out to him, "Did you see that? It was perfect!"

"Sure was nice, son," Mr. E shouted back.

"Dad," Norm stopped still and gazed over at his father, "Do you think I can someday play in the NFL?"

Without skipping a beat Mr. E quipped back, "You can do, have and achieve anything you put your mind to, never forget."

Without hesitation, Norm turned back to us all, yelled out to Eddie, "Hurry up off the ground, Spankie [Eddie's nickname], and let's kick this ball off to these two jokers." (The jokers, of course, were JoJo and me.)

As the years of my childhood hurtled forward, there were many scenes like this with my friend Norman and his passion for football, but the significance of it all began to come perfectly clear about seven years later.

We were all in college and home for Thanksgiving break. Norm and I met up at the local tavern, Hutley's, and were just sipping our first beer (yes, the drinking age was 18 back then), and we were talking over the top of one another trying to get all of our college experiences to date off of our chests, when all of a sudden an old high school classmate interrupted us with, "Hey there guys, how you doing?"

We both stopped and looked up as he peered down at us sitting at the table. "How is college going?" he added.

"Great." we both quickly responded, eager to get back to our conversation.

"Hey," he interrupted us again, yelling over the music while peering down at my friend Norm, "I heard you are playing football at Maryland."

"Yes, as a matter of fact I am. In fact, I was fortunate enough to get a full scholarship." Norm replied.

"Nice, good for you," the kid quipped back, "But hey," he went on, "you don't still have that crazy dream about becoming a quarterback in the NFL, do you?"

Norm, perturbed by the interruption but now with a look of agitation in his eyes, stopped, looked up from his chair and confidently said with a forced smile, "Well as a matter of fact, I do."

Without skipping a beat, the classmate looked at Norm and said, "You know only one in a million make it to the pros, never mind becoming an NFL quarterback."

To which Norm, still seated, rolled his eyes at the kid and calmly replied, "Why don't you take your beer and drink elsewhere..."

Again, the kid spewed on, "Hey, all I'm trying to say is that you were pretty darn good in high school, but college and the pros are not nearly the same. Besides..." The young man, who was now taking his life into his own hands but I am quite sure didn't know it, pushed on. "You're left handed and the overwhelming majority of the quarterbacks in the NFL are right handed."

This was the last thing the kid said as Norm calmly stood up, a towering 6' 5" young man similar to the stature of his dad, and said with the look of death in his eyes and a loud, forceful command, "I told you, take your beer and leave, now!"

With a severe look of shock and awe on his face, the classmate snatched his beer from the edge of the table where he placed it earlier, wisely I might add, and walked away. Almost without skipping a beat Norm sat back in his chair and immediately began to engage back into our original conversation...

Until I stopped him and said, "That was a little abrupt and harsh to that guy, don't you think?"

"What do you mean?" he said as he thrust forward in his chair.

"I just think you were rude as all get-out to that guy," I exclaimed.

"What the heck do you mean, Joey?" (Almost everyone who grew up in Long Island was given an "ie" or an "ey" at the end of their name.) "I didn't do a damn thing harsh, rude or wrong."

"Oh, you didn't?" I said back, with the look of a little bit of judgment mixed with some curiosity.

"No!" he said. "Let me ask you something, Joey. In all the years we have known each other and the countless hours we have hung out together, have you ever, ever said anything similar to what that guy just said to me?"

"Well no, of course not." I said.

"Yeah, and how about Eddie or JoJo, have you ever heard them say anything like that to me?"

"No, never," I said.

"And how about the high school football coach, have you ever heard him utter those words?"

"No." I said.

"And how about my sisters, Robin or Susan, have you ever heard it from them?"

Again I replied, "No."

"And how about my Dad, did you ever hear my Dad say these words or any other words even remotely similar to them my entire life?"

"Absolutely not," I said sternly.

"THEN WHO THE HELL IS HE? WHO IS THIS GUY TO SAY THAT TO ME!"

I will never forget that evening. Furthermore, I would love to tell you that at the ripe age of nineteen I comprehended what had just taken place that night, but it was not until about four years later that it all became clear...that is when my lifelong friend, Norman Julius Esiason (much better known by the childhood nickname "Boomer" given to him by his family from his constant kicking while inside of his mother's womb), was drafted into the NFL to play quarterback for the Cincinnati Bengals. That, by the way, is why I was sitting in the stands at Joe Robbie Stadium at Super Bowl XXIII, the day the 49ers beat the Bengals in the last few moments of the game!

You see, when my "bro" Boomer Swaggered his way to the Super Bowl, he took me and all the people he loved to the place where those with Swagger go...the Big Game.

My lifelong friend Boomer amassed a combined college and NFL list of accomplishments that includes:

As a Maryland Terp:
- He set 17 school records and led his team to the ACC title and the Citrus Bowl in 1983.
- Esiason completed 461 of 850 passes (54.2 percent) for 6,169 yards and 42 touchdowns with 27 interceptions.
- He was a two-time honorable mention All-American in 1982 and 1983.
- In his final home game, he threw two third-quarter touchdown passes to lead a comeback victory over No. 3 North Carolina to seal the ACC title.
- Esiason graduated with a B.A. in 1984 and received the Distinguished Alumnus Award in 1999.

And as an NFL Quarterback:
- He led the Cincinnati Bengals to the AFC Championship in 1988.
- He earned the league's Most Valuable Player award in 1988.
- Esiason also led the AFC in passing in both 1988 and 1989.

- Boomer was named to four Pro Bowl games (1986, 1988, 1989, 1993).
- He holds several NFL career records for left-handed quarterbacks, including most touchdown passes (247), passing yards (37,920), and completions (2,969).
- And among his many accomplishments, his most crowning was leading the Cincinnati Bengals to Super Bowl XXIII, by far one of the most exciting and memorable super bowls in NFL history (to which he made sure all of his family members and childhood best friends accompanied him, to share in his success).
- Upon his retirement in 1997, he was among the most prolific quarterbacks in NFL history, finishing in the top 10 in many statistical categories.

As I look back fondly over all those years, there are truly no surprises in the long list of goals, achievements and life dreams realized by Boomer. Even when we were young children, it was clear to see that it was not simply his athletic skills that led to his success; Boomer had a completely different set of beliefs from the majority of people you and I meet...a set of **core governing beliefs** that emitted from him then and are still easy to see to this day, such as initiative, self-reliance, fearlessness, courage, persistence, tenacity, and imagination—the very same traits found in all successful people. These are the traits readily seen in all people with Swagger.

Simply put, Boomer marches to the beat of a different drum, a rhythm that germinates from a distinct set of beliefs that conspire together each day into a mindset that guides his decisions, drive his actions and fuel his ability to create and achieve results...extremely successful results. Boomer has a **Swagger-Set**!

One needs only to engage in a five-minute chat with my friend Boomer to feel the heat and capture the light that radiates from everything he thinks, says and does. The difference in the way Boomer thinks, reasons and behaves is undeniable, and so is the long list of personal and professional triumphs that mark his life's journey.

An Organized Mind—The Core Ingredients to Building a Swagger-Set

My friend Boomer and the other people with Swagger you and I have been blessed throughout life to study, meet and possibly befriend, have a mindset that is organized by and rooted in beliefs that are different from the overwhelming majority of people in society.

As a personal participant in this gift called life, as a sales professional and possibly as a current and/or future leader of others in your leadership roles (parent, coach, teacher, manager), imagine what you could accomplish and what you could help others (your children, co-workers, direct reports) achieve if you could systematically identify, develop and organize the core beliefs that embody the Mindset of people with Swagger! What would you dare to dream? What would you risk to achieve? And how would it impact your ability to help those you lead reach for the stars!

The exhilarating news is that we are all born with the **potential** to grow, change and sculpt ourselves into people who live, love, and sell with Swagger by organizing our mindset around the same set of core governing beliefs…the caliber of beliefs that serve as the precursor to the mastery of all skills and talents needed for professional and personal success!

All skills, talent and abilities are first born in the seed of a burning desire, fueled by a set of core beliefs, cradled in faith.

Mind Over 'Matter'

I want you to see that the "Mind" makes, shapes and defines "Matter," not the other way around. On an individual level it is not where you are born, nor where you live, or whether you have money or resources, that dictates the results and success you will achieve in life. On an institutional/organizational level, it is not a Matter of your product, service, competition, the economy, or the market that controls your sales success…for all of these things are simply Matter, and Matter, as defined by Webster's Dictionary, is "a situation, state, affair or business."

What *matters*, what really always matters is the mindset that each of us brings to each situation, circumstance, event…whether these conditions are positive and conducive for success or not. It's starting to sound a lot like the Urban Dictionary's definition of Swagger we discussed earlier, isn't it?

"How one presents him or herself to the world. Swagger is shown from how a person handles a situation."

Situations, circumstances and events can slow us down, can temporarily detain us from achieving the results we covet in our heart; but they cannot stop us from the progressive realization of the things we want to achieve or the life we commit to build.

Many young children growing up have the thought impulse to become a professional athlete, but what caused a boy named Boomer Esiason to grow up and become a great NFL quarterback while so many others fall short?

Speaking of short, for those who would naively say size and natural ability were the reasons for Boomer's success, what enables a child with a dream on a Baltimore school playground, who at full maturity grew to the ripe height of 5'4", to stick with his dream and become an NBA star known as Muggsy Bogues? Surely he, like my lifelong friend Boomer, was told he was too slow or too short or that few ever make it into the NBA.

What enables a young girl from Rochester, New York with nothing more than hope and a dream, to grow up and become one of the greatest women ever to play the game of soccer? If we want to stick with the dominant mental paradigm that Matter (circumstance, situations, events) yields results, surely there are places in the country where the weather conditions are favorable and children can play, practice and dream all year long outdoors to perfect their soccer skills. Not a reality for Abby Wambach, key player of the Olympic gold medalist team, who was named WUSA Rookie of the Year and Most Valuable Player in 2002, and went on to lead the US team to Olympic gold not once, but twice. Abby learned soccer on the frozen fields of upstate New York.

How about outside the genre of sports and into the world of engineering and science...Thomas Edison was not born into a family of wealth, stature or parents that were scientists and/or inventors. He surely encountered endless setbacks and discouraging obstacles of Matter, including conducting a legendary 9,999 failed experiments before finally creating the incandescent light bulb that changed the world...no doubt, Edison was told often by others around him that the light bulb and the long list of 1,092 other inventions he was responsible for creating (including cement, the phonograph, curling iron, the battery, and many others) were not possible. Yet he chose to believe, act and achieve results anyway! His results created far more than personal wealth; they changed the world.

On an institutional level, what enabled an icon like Steve Jobs to believe, embrace and act on a future for himself and his company, Apple; that when it was all said and he was all done with his life's work, it would be recognized as one of the greatest corporate accomplishments in the history of the capitalist system—and change the way the world looks at computers and communication forever? Surely there were setbacks, failures, and a long line of people to tell him along the way that he could not, would not succeed...but he did.

In fact, wasn't Steve Jobs fired once from Apple?

Or how about CEO legends, such as Jack Welch from GE or Lee Iacocca from Chrysler, who took the reins of struggling behemoths and transformed them into viable entities that still thrive to this day? Surely it was not because they were given the reins to the next Secretariat. Candidly, it was quite the opposite...these companies might have found their way to the glue factory (so to speak) if it were not for leaders who understood that it was the "mind that matters," not the other way around.

But what is it specifically about the minds of successful men and women that consistently causes them to succeed, while the majority of others fail when presented with similar opportunities or confronted with similar challenges, obstacles and setbacks?

Much more than simply showcasing these leaders' triumphs and doting on their successes, you are about to discover exactly why the people with Swagger you have studied or personally observed are able to consistently "Bend Matter" and achieve successful results when an overwhelming majority of others would, could and do fail.

History documents these icons most often by listing their accomplishments and speaking of the virtues and traits that enabled their success. These are the very same leadership traits mentioned, observed, and identified in every book, program, class and discussion on successful people.

However, this is where the majority of analysis and the study of successful people starts and ends. The piece that is missing is the identification of the core governing beliefs from which all these traits germinate.

Human potential is accessed and unleashed through a set of core governing beliefs, and people with Swagger—you know those successful people; you read about, study, work with, grew up with them —possess a mindset which is organized and built upon these beliefs.

So what are these core beliefs?

How many core beliefs are there?

Can you and I really see, refine and shape these beliefs within ourselves?

Can you create ultimate sales career security and abundance by building these beliefs into a Swagger-Set?

Is it possible to use this Swagger-Set to create the results you want in every area of your life?

Can we see, refine and shape these core beliefs in others?

And, if we could, what would be possible?

Can you imagine institutionalizing this approach to teaching skills and applying it to create a championship sales team, engineering team, customer service team, and/or an entire company?

Some say you can…some say you can't…I say that both are just a "matter of the mind" and therefore up to you to decide.

Swagenitions:

- Swagger-Set = is a collection of core beliefs, a Mindset
- Traits = the outward projection of inner beliefs

Chapter 1:

SWAGGER-SET: A MINDSET COMPRISED OF OPTIMAL BELIEFS

As famous author and philosopher James Allen—author of one of the best self-help books ever written, *As a Man Thinketh*, and a subsequently published companion version, *As a Woman Thinketh*—once profoundly stated, "Circumstance does not make the man; it reveals him to himself."

In other words, what James Allen and countless other philosophers, poets, spiritual leaders or those we often reference as enlightened, want us all to recognize is that we habitually behave—act/react—based upon who we truly are. And who we are is the summation of what we have come to believe. As such, you can always tell what kind of timber a person is made of, not by what they say in situations and circumstances, but by how they actually move. We move in accordance with our beliefs; and we do so not because we want to but because we have to. Our actions are always subservient to our beliefs.

As a leader of "self" and as a leader of others, I know that this simple truth, this wisdom of the ages, is critical to recognize and understand. The collaboration of **optimal core beliefs—the Swagger-Set**—makes us capable of achieving results. Conversely, those who do not have Swagger, those who cling to **inferior beliefs**, are rendered incapable of achieving the results they seek.

Neither chance nor circumstance is the maker and molder of your destiny. How you Swagger—meaning how you act and/or react to life's situations and events—controls your propensity for success, dictates your actual results and defines your past as well as your future.

Trigger Traits—the Outward Reflection of Optimal Core Beliefs

The Trigger Traits found in all successful sales professionals and all people with Swagger are one in the same. The corporate leaders who participated in the focus group I described earlier gave us the list of these traits (Imaginative, Creative, Positive, Confident, Driven, Motivated, Self-Starters, Tenacious, Persistent, Resilient, Adaptable, Risk Tolerant, Fearless, Courageous, Committed, and Goal-Directed). You can test this truth by taking any successful person throughout history and he or she will embody this list. In fact, you can take any person with Swagger that you know, superimpose his or her name at the top of this list of trigger traits, and that person, too, will embody most if not all of these traits. We all recognize and know this to be true.

But why?

The simple answer is that all traits are an outward reflection of our inner beliefs. As such, Core Beliefs—built and organized around an understanding of human potential and how to harness it—germinate traits that trigger the ideal action and/or reaction to events, situations and circumstances as we walk through life.

If you know what you are looking for, you can readily see these traits in others. You can surely feel the heat that emanates from people who possess a set of organized optimal beliefs that imbue a Swagger-Set capable of achieving whatever result they dare to dream. The challenge is that most individuals and people in leadership positions across society's institutions are unaware that these powerful and virtuous traits can be cultivated. Most people do not know that they can build and refine the core beliefs from which these traits germinate. I sincerely believe that this prior statement will be the next generation of how trainers, educators and leaders approach both adult and child learning over the next 100 years and beyond.

For individuals who develop these core beliefs within themselves, the possibilities for personal and professional success are endless. For those who internalize these beliefs and eventually lead others to do the same, the positive impact and change for good they can help create in the lives of others (and within entire teams, organizations and institutions) is profound.

As a young man fresh out of school, I was helped to identify these core beliefs and tirelessly mentored to internalize them by my friend Randy. A few years later, I was promoted to sales management, where I was taught how to help others construct and refine those same core beliefs into a Swagger-Set that captured awards by my new hires that included Sales Rookie of the Year, President's Club Awards and a similar progression of promotions into upper management positions. The Swagger-Set is a formula I went on to perfect and teach to salespeople across industry with profound impact and results.

Take a turn of the page with me now and I will explain exactly what these five beliefs are that radiate the trigger traits to success vs. the trigger traits to failure.

Chapter 5:

UNLOCKING YOUR SWAGGER: IS THERE A MASTER KEY?

Dear Joe:

Many thanks for your support this year. It proved to be a successful year for me. There were many people cheering me on throughout the year. You were one of those people.

When I arrived home last Thursday night following the Sales Event, I asked my son and husband to lie down on the bed and read aloud the sign taped to the ceiling. The sign listed my desired income and the word "TOP." When I placed that sign on the ceiling above my bed at the beginning of the year, I recall thinking, "I must be crazy." It was the first and last thing I saw morning after morning and night after night.

When both Zach and Steve finished reading it out loud, I showed them the Top Performer plaque presented to me just hours earlier in Cleveland. Steve already knew that I had surpassed the income goal. I don't suppose I have to tell you that those two guys are now believers!

It is sort of crazy and humorous, but it is real! Thank you for your inspiration. You encouraged me to move beyond the imaginary line that I previously thought only a select few had the ability to cross.

Only good things to you...

Cordially,

Top Health Insurance Company

This letter, written and given to me by Sharon, is not an exception or rare occurrence. It is the reaction and sentiment my extraordinary team of talented trainers and I have received weekly from business professionals for more than two and a half decades.

When I first met Sharon, it was at the very beginning of a long-term working relationship with the top health insurance company in Ohio. Sharon was in customer service at the time, but set her sights on earning a position on the sales team, and set her internal compass on becoming the number one sales person in the company.

A few brief years later, Sharon's dream became reality...but not simply because of some sales skill, technique, strategy or process I taught her. Her dream became a progressive realization in a short period of time because of the refinement and alignment of her core beliefs first. Sharon learned how to Swagger-Sell.

How did Sharon make this rapid ascent to the top a reality? The answer was the same for Sharon as it is for you, me, and anyone who rises to the pinnacle of success in their career and in life: belief! Yes, Sharon needed to learn and develop the core fundamental skills of sales to succeed, but as you now know, all skills, all abilities are **first** born in the seed of desire; and all desire germinates from belief. Not just any belief, however; a set of core governing beliefs from which all things become possible: a Swagger-Set.

At the time of Sharon's promotion into sales and the declaration of her goal to become number one, there were some who bet against her achieving this dream. However, they bet wrong, because they were looking at who she was, not at who she believed she could become.

Unfortunately the list is infinite of those who, at one time, had a dream that was squelched and smothered by ignorance—ignorance they embraced about life, the world, and their potential to achieve their dreams before they even got started.

These "unsung somebodies" remain on the list of "nobodies" because they failed to learn how to develop a Swagger-Set first. They failed to systematically create the result—the life—they wanted to have, professionally and personally, because they failed to embark on the journey by way of mindset change, first.

Think about how many dreams/goals you have let go, allowed to pass you by, or placed on hold.

Think about others you know who are possibly right next to you, who have done or are doing the same.

The *failure to launch*, the *failure to execute*, the *failure to master fundamental skills*, and the *failure to follow a process/plan* that will surely lead to success...all these common things are not the problem, they are merely the symptoms of the problem.

The root cause of the problem is a mindset devoid of the core governing beliefs that imbue faith and the ability to act. For these people, their mindset is organized around limiting beliefs that perpetuate traits that enable failure to grow and thrive; for there can be no Swagger in a mind imprisoned by mental walls constructed out of flawed beliefs.

Traits such as these perpetuate failure:

- Indifference
- Negative
- Defeatist
- Fearful
- Lack of Confidence
- Dependent
- Scarcity Mentality

- Unimaginative
- Easily discouraged
- Inability to adapt/change and grow
- Wavering
- Trapped by Inertia
- Lack of motivation
- Lack of personal responsibility

The Master Key

The Swagger-Set is a success mindset, the one I discovered and perfected that unlocks sales professionals, teams, and entire companies 100 percent of the time. You read that correctly: 100 percent of the time.

It's based on five core governing beliefs, which are reflected outwardly by the trigger traits of success we've talked about earlier. These five core governing beliefs unlock people, *all* people, and enable them to Swagger Sell their way through life.

Traits such as these perpetuate success:

- Creative
- Positive
- Resilient
- Courageous
- Confident
- Self-Reliant
- Abundant Mentality

- Imaginative
- Persistent
- Adaptive
- Determined
- Takes Initiative
- Self-Motivated
- Accepts Personal Responsibility

Warning

In a moment I am going to reveal to you these five core governing beliefs. However, before I do, I must warn you of a few things:

1. As you read these core governing beliefs your "voice" (yes, we don't like to admit it but we all talk to ourselves) will speak loud and clear to you when you agree (which means it is already a core belief you possess), and it will speak to you loud and clear when you disagree (which means you have a core belief that is juxtaposed/opposite to what I am explaining). The most important thing to remember is that neither you nor I are right or wrong; it is just who we are, what we believe right now. However, the most important point of your mental dialogue is not to discern who is right or wrong, because the internal mental dialogue is not between us, it is between you and the results you want to achieve in your sales career and life.
2. I must also warn you that this part and the remainder of our dialogue within this book will alter and change the way you see yourself, others and the world around you. Forever...

Are you ready? Here we go ...

Chapter 6:

SWAGGER-SET: A MIND MATRIX COMPRISED OF FIVE CORE BELIEFS

Comprised in this chapter are the five Core Beliefs I have carefully and strategically built and refined in those I have coached to reach their full potential in sales and in life. It is what I have come to call the master key to unlock every individual, team and entire organization I have ever had the distinct honor and pleasure to work with—100% of the time. Yes, I have made the bold claim "100% of the time" again, and you are about to discover exactly why!

For your ease of read and for future reference I have organized the discussion of each Core Belief with three guiding questions:

- What does this mean?
- What does a sales career/life fueled by this Core Belief look like?
- How do you apply this Belief?

For as Confucius once stated, "The answers are always found from asking the right questions."

Swagger-Set Core Belief #1: You Have the Power to Create

What Does This Mean?

You and I have been given the gift of life, and the very essence of this gift is our power to create. Create a life of dreams and their accomplishment. Elephants can't create, dogs can't create, orangutans can't create…but you and I can! You and I, like Edison, Einstein, Jordan, Jobs, DiCaprio, Esiason, Bogues, King and every and any person with Swagger you have studied, worked with, befriended, know or have known, all have the power to create. All people with Swagger move through life with this awareness, this core belief. And they believe it deeply, to their very core.

As such, they use this gift every day, week, month and year to envision the results, the outcomes, to the life they seek. They do not believe this somewhat and apply it periodically; they live their entire lives this way and see life through this prism. They envision what they want in their inner world (through the faculties of their imagination) and maintain their vision until…

…Until that which they create in their inner world manifests into reality in their outer world.

Edison did not have the light bulb in his hand and then started thinking about it, any more than Boomer Esiason woke up an NFL quarterback and then started thinking/dreaming about playing the game.

The simple truth for Edison, Esiason, Jobs, and for you or me is this: All results, all accomplishments start and germinate from one place: **a core belief in our ability to create!**

What does a sales career/life fueled by this Core Belief look like?

Traits like inventiveness, creativity or imagination all germinate from the belief in our innate ability to create. Now that it has been revealed, it is not difficult to see why icons throughout history and the people you know who have Swagger possess this trait in abundance. They understand this, they believe it and as such, they act in accordance to this belief and thereby create every day. Their core belief in their ability to create hides in plain sight because it is easily observed in their daily behaviors/traits.

This is why our greatest leaders throughout history are often referred to as dreamers. However, it would be nice if rather than simply acknowledging them as dreamers, we were all helped to see why they possessed this trait. It is a gift we all receive at birth. It is a refined filament of human potential consistently cited in our formal study of successful people in school, such as Thomas Edison, the Wright brothers, Ronald Reagan, John F. Kennedy, Mother Theresa. They were dreamers, innovators, and creators, and now you know why. They possess the same gift that you have: The Power To Create.

How do you apply this belief?

What is that old saying? Seeing is believing—or is it believing is seeing...or are they both the same within the confines of the human mind?

What does a sales career/life look like without this core belief? People whose careers and lives are devoid of this truth and awareness are unwilling and unable to envision themselves as a master of the sales skills (process) essential to their success. This inability to first imagine themselves bigger, better, skilled and capable defeats them before they even get started. Why? Because we cannot and will not become what we do not imagine and create in our own mind, first!

Sharon dreamt of being number one, Boomer dreamt of being an NFL quarterback, Steve Jobs dreamt of changing the world with technology. All people who live a life of results embrace and apply their ability—the same ability you have—to create. They created the image of what they wanted to do, have and become, and they never mentally let go of it.

Sharon said, "It was the first and last thing I would see every day." Boomer said, "Who the hell is he to tell me I can't?" Jobs said to John Scully, CEO of Pepsi: "Do you want to sell sugar water the rest of your life, or do you want to come with me and change the world?"

What is important to embrace, internalize and apply is that you not only have the power to create, you must use it. People with Swagger do it every day. A doctor becomes a doctor because one day he or she began to think and dream about becoming a doctor. A lawyer becomes a lawyer because one day, he or she began to envision himself or herself as a lawyer. The #1 salesperson and the other massively successful sales professionals with Swagger all started their journey to the top in their mind's eye, by seeing themselves as the best, first.

Swagger-Set Core Belief #2: You Have Unlimited Potential

What does this mean?

All people who have Swagger come to the understanding that they have unlimited potential to grow and master whatever abilities they need in order to make their dreams reality.

Once again, Edison was not a great inventor first, and then began to develop the skills, abilities and mastery of the techniques/strategies of inventing. It had to be, and it was, the other way around.

My lifelong friend, Boomer Esiason, did not get drafted into the NFL and then develop the skills, abilities and mastery of techniques/ strategies of a great quarterback on the day he was drafted into the NFL. He had to become it first; and JoJo, Eddie and I have the bodily scars to prove he worked on it, first.

The same is true of people who become a great coach like Rick Pitino of Louisville, or John Wooden from UCLA, or Vince Lombardi from the Green Bay Packers; a great CEO like Jack Welch or Lee Iacocca; or a top sales person, customer service representative, the best engineer, the best manager/supervisor; or even a great mom, dad, sibling or friend.

These folks, and all people with Swagger, recognize one simple universal truth: **"Before you can have the things you dream of, you must become the person capable of making your dream a reality."** But in order to become, you must believe you can. You must come to the understanding/recognition that you can refine yourself, improve yourself, and evolve yourself into the talented and gifted person you were born to be.

Far too many among us fail to recognize their unlimited potential to evolve, grow and change, and instead set limits on their goals and dreams in life. As such, they fail to capture the abundance life has to offer, because they fail to recognize the abundance within themselves.

What does a sales career/life fueled by this core belief look like?

All individuals who reach the pinnacle of success, all those who lead others to greatness, do so from the recognition and progressive realization of their full potential.

It is not difficult to see that people who possess trigger traits such as the willingness to try new things, adapt, learn from failure, dream grand dreams, and set lofty goals do so because they envision a future not based on who they are, but based on who they know they can and will become.

For some, you may say my exuberance is a little over the top. However, I cannot be exuberant enough.

Big dreams, big goals, big accomplishments, big results do not come from the handiwork of small, unevolved, underdeveloped people. Big successes come from Big People, and the universal precursor to becoming Big is Belief: *Belief about your potential to change, grow and become more tomorrow than you are today.* Ultimately in order to fill your personal sales cup with results till it runneth over, you must enshrine in your mind that you have unlimited potential to grow, change and become whatever you must to command success.

How do you apply this belief?

Each time I have trained, coached and nurtured a new salesperson's rapid assent to peak performer, rookie of the year, President's Club, or top performer, I have helped them to succeed by helping them to recognize both the need and ability to tap into more of their potential, first. Each and every time I have helped a tenured, underperforming salesperson or an average-level producer to break out and ascend to the stature of top producer, it has been accomplished by helping them to recognize and accept personal responsibility to invest in themselves— to develop and/or refine their skills. I help them embrace this clear and demonstrable shift in behavior by leading them to recognize that "before they can have, they must become—but before they can become, they must believe that they have the unlimited and untapped personal potential to do so."

None of us were born riding a bicycle, walking, talking—these are all talents bestowed within us in the form of potential. Neither are we born with the mastery of prospecting, qualifying or any of the other sales skills we need to break out and rise to the pinnacle of sales success! These selling skills—like all talents—lie dormant within us in the form of potential until we choose to awaken and master them.

Swagger-Set Core Belief #3: Results are a Function of Cause and Effect

What does this mean?

What makes the forces of nature and the beauty of the earth so perfect, so precise and so predictable? These things, like all things, are governed by the law of cause and effect. The sun rises in the east and it surely sets in the west not three days or four days a week—it does it that way every day, seven days of the week, because the universe is governed by the law of cause and effect.

As we all learned in eighth grade science, *for every action there is an equal and opposite reaction*. It was taught to us all by Sir Isaac Newton as the first law of physics.

However, this is not a discussion on science; this is a life-altering discussion on how to become a person with Swagger in the game of life. As such, it is important to recognize all people with Swagger awaken to the awareness and utter belief—the Core Governing Belief—that results are not crafted and captured from random plans, random strategies, or random actions…they are built and progressively realized from deliberate action.

Why is this so important to comprehend and embrace? Why is embedding this belief so important to the Swagger-Set mental lexicon? Simply put, it prevents you and me from wasting countless hours, days, months and even years trying to reach goals or fulfill dreams based upon lotions, potions and lies. Instead, we can focus our time, energy and actions on the skill refinement, best practices, strategies, processes, and plans that consistently create **success**! And as we illustrated earlier in the Swagger Success Model, success is defined by the **Results** you seek!

What does a career/life fueled by this core belief look like?

It is staggering to me how many times I have met with salespeople seeking results yet are in denial or oblivious to the simple truth that life will not give them their bounty by following just any plan or rules that they wish to follow. The universe will only reveal and give up her treasures to those men and women who take the time to isolate the right plan, the proper law that rules…The Law of Cause and Effect.

I could provide you with countless examples to help you anchor this Core Governing Belief, but I always bring clarity to my students by asking a few simple questions:

"How many people here ever set a goal to improve their personal finances? Let me see a show of hands!"

Almost always, 100% of the hands swing up. I then say, "Yes, we all have. And what is typically the first thing we do when we want to improve in any given area? We read a few books on the subject. However, inevitably when we get about halfway through the second and definitely by the third book, we realize that each book on the subject of personal finance all say what?"

My students always pause for a moment, but then almost in complete unison respond, "They all say the same thing."

To which I respond, "Correct! The books all say the key to financial stability, strength, and ultimately independence comes down to a few key things." These things include:

- Establish and follow a personal budget.
- Live below your means.
- Declare war on all personal debt.
- Recognize that a part of all you earn is yours to keep forever.

- Once you save, get some coveralls on your money and get it working for you through prudent investing.
- Use debt sparingly, if at all.
- Adopt a "save and buy" mentality.

"Ultimately we all know that if we embrace and execute these strategies we will achieve the result we seek—**financial success**."

To further anchor the point and achieve buy-in from my students regarding the belief that *results are a function of cause and effect*, I immediately follow up with another powerful example:

"If you and I want to improve our physical health, we may read one or two books, perhaps a few articles, but inevitably after a few reads we realize what?"

The groups always respond with vigor now, "They all say the same thing!"

To which I immediately respond, "What do they say?" Their responses are always close to exactly this:

- Eat plenty of protein, avoid sugars/carbs and fat.
- Take vitamins.
- Drink 8-10 glasses of water per day (always a tough one for people on the go).
- Get a minimum of 7-8 hours of sleep per night.
- Exercise at least one hour a day; a minimum of 30-45 minutes of which should be aerobic exercise.

It's clear that the law of cause and effect is applicable to achieving powerful results in finances and physical health. However, it is important to recognize that it is applicable to everything, including becoming a top producing sales person, a peak performing customer service representative, a great manager/leader, or even a terrific friend, father or mother.

No matter what outcome, what result you and I are looking to accomplish in life, it is always a matter of cause and effect…always!

How do you apply this belief?

Helping to establish and anchor the core belief of cause and effect, at times, has been difficult for individual contributors, teams, divisions and entire companies with whom my associates and I have had the distinct honor and pleasure to work with. But the question is why?

The answer is this: The core governing belief that results are a function of cause and effect germinates one of the most important traits of all—**personal responsibility**.

Ultimately when we analyze the stature and station of the life we have, and compare it to the results of the life we seek through the prism of cause and effect, there are no excuses.

We either take the actions we need to get the results we dream about...or we do not!

As a new or tenured sales representative, you can create the vision and the goal of becoming the rookie of the year, a top producer or even the #1 producer in your organization. However, if you fail to isolate the exact skills, best practices and strategies of those that achieve these heights of success and instead attempt to wish for your success by only mastering some selling skills and some strategies, you will certainly fail.

For decades, I have observed sales professionals haphazardly set their goals—then focus only on developing the sales skills and strategies essential to their success that they like, are comfortable with, or that come easily to them. Theirs is a mind unable to Swagger because it is devoid of the awareness that their results are completely dependent on what they do or fail to do each day. If this is not corrected and redirected, it is the sure-fire recipe for failure.

As a leader and performance development expert, I have helped scores of salespeople (new or tenured) break free of this thinking by simply and respectfully asking, "Since when does doing only the things you like to do, are comfortable doing, or that come easily to you, have anything to do with your success?"

Every person I speak with and help with this simple question knows in their heart and from personal performance history—in anything—

that it has not helped. In fact, their denial and defiance of this simple truth has held them back.

Swagger-Set Core Belief #4: Self-Esteem/Self-Efficacy

What does this mean?

The understanding, appreciation, and the unconditional love/respect of "self" is omnipotent to the core governing beliefs that serve as the power plant of a Swagger mindset. The genre of personal self-help and the "thought leaders" that paved the path into the consciousness of the public domain like Norman Vincent Peele, Maxwell Maltz, Napoleon Hill, James Allen, Viktor Frankl, Paul J. Meyer, and W. Clement Stone—to name several of the true greats—often wrote and talked about the importance of self-esteem/self-efficacy. Many of them reference this awareness as the discovery of the "Other Self."

In essence, this reference to the "Other Self" is about an individual's discovery and subsequent change in awareness regarding both their worthiness and propensity to achieve. This reference is not only true, but it's a critical element in the construction of a mindset capable of delivering positive and tangible results in any and all areas of life. It is a critical component of the Swagger-Set!

Countless studies conclude that the quantity and quality of success an individual achieves in life is directly and completely attributable to the strength, integrity, and fortitude of their belief about "Self."

And when it comes to the harmonic ecosystem of the Swagger-Set, it is a matter of helping individuals understand how their self-esteem was formed and how it positively or negatively shapes their self-efficacy (meaning their belief about their ability to master skills, situations, and things).

So much of our ability to consistently act with initiative, live with self-reliance, cope with change, learn through failure, overcome setbacks/obstacles, and thereby face all of life's opportunities and challenges with supreme confidence and faith comes down to self-esteem and self-efficacy. Simply put, building the proper core belief about "self" provides the fertile mental ground needed for the seeds of these traits to germinate and open into a full bloom.

What does a career/life fueled by this core belief look like?

Sales talent with strong self-esteem and self-efficacy are able to embrace core selling skills and persistently refine them into excellence. They can execute best practices and strategies until they are perfected, because they are both open and able to accept the negative feedback that comes hand in hand with mastery. New or tenured salespeople with strong self-esteem thereby exude a positive, resilient, persistent and adaptable demeanor, and it consistently propels them to the top.

Sales talent that lack this core component of the Swagger-Set are resistant to change, lack confidence and an ability to adapt, focus on problems rather than solutions, find it extremely difficult to accept negative feedback, and are thereby shackled by the tethers of underperformance.

How do you apply this belief?

Although there are many avenues I could go down to describe how to help you shape and refine this core belief of self-esteem/self-efficacy, there is one technique which was given to me at twenty-one by my mentor that my organization and I have given to hundreds of thousands throughout the years. The technique uses three simple questions each time you look to refine a new skill or process:

• What did I do right?
• What did I do wrong?
• What will I refine or do differently next time?

Anytime we bust a move to master a skill we need in order to become the best, we will inevitably receive negative feedback. For just about every skill or ability you have acquired, you have encountered and endured negative feedback on the road to mastery. The bumped head and/or stitches received by the toddler learning to walk, the skinned knees and broken bones dealt to the child learning to ride a bicycle, or the lost sales and income to the salesperson who blows up a sales opportunity—it is always the same. The attempt to execute creates both positive and negative feedback, and usually at the beginning, it is a great deal of negative feedback. It's the kind of negative feedback that can be crushing when received by those whose confidence, self-efficacy and belief in "self" is weak and unevolved.

These three simple questions give us the mental shield we need by teaching and enabling us to see that **feedback is not good or bad, it just is; all that matters is what we learn from it.**

Swagger-Set Core Belief #5: Your Fear is Your Friend

What does this mean?

I have witnessed nothing more debilitating or more preventative to an individual's ability to obtain results in their sales career and personal life than their ill-fated belief(s) about their fears, and the internal comfort zones they harbor that cause them.

In each area of life, the true abundance and pleasures of the life we seek are often squandered away because of a failure to formulate the optimal beliefs/awareness regarding our fears and comfort zones.

The friendships and relationships that could have been but never were, all due to the mental misrepresentation of fear; the personal problems never addressed; the physical ailments that could have been avoided, prevented or cured; the games, hobbies, adventures never played and/or never explored; the career opportunities never captured or exploited; the incredible business idea never acted upon; the dreams that were left dormant within the confines of our mind… all of these limiting twists of fate and countless others could have been overcome and transformed through faith…faith in the belief that our **fear is our friend.**

What does a career/life fueled by this core belief look like?

It is important to recognize that people with sales Swagger are not devoid of fear each day as they act on their ideas and turn their dreams into results, any more than the concept of darkness can exist without the light. The simple truth is that people with Swagger come to recognize and understand that the emotion of fear is always "present" on the path to achievement of anything.

But the question is why? Why is fear always front and center on the stage of the life we want to produce?

To answer this critical question, we must isolate the root cause or source of all fear. The great news is that there are two main sources that grip the soul with fear, and once you understand them, the newfound awareness will enable you to unshackle this grip forever.

1. **Fear is caused by the unknown**...anytime we attempt to try or do something for the very first time, the emotion of fear fills and consumes the mind. The good news is that this instinct enabled our predecessors, like the caveman, to stop and think before they simply stepped off a 40-foot cliff. Because the law of gravity would have surely made the law of cause and effect easy to see and believe...meaning that if you step off a 40-foot cliff, you will, most likely, die when you hit the ground.

   However, in the modern world, when it comes to taking the steps we need to make our dreams and goals a reality, there are few, if any, unknowns. Therefore our containment and mastery of fear is within reach when combined with the second insight...

2. **The emotion of fear is evoked when we are confronted with our own unique set of comfort zones.** This second facet of fear is critical to understand, but most people go through their entire lives never defining or understanding the concept of comfort zones—and, more importantly, learning how to recognize their own comfort zones. This is in spite of the fact that we all have comfort zones—and we have all experienced the wall of fear they emit when we come up against one.

   So, what is a comfort zone? Simply put, a comfort zone is the imaginary line in our mind's eye that we encounter whenever we come to the mental crossroad of *what we believe we are capable of doing and what we believe we are not capable of doing.*

However, we have already learned in Swagger-Set Core Belief #2 that we have what kind of potential? That's right, "Unlimited Potential." We each possess unlimited potential to grow, master and execute whatever skill, talent and plan we need to achieve the result we seek. This is the simple truth!

How do you apply this belief?

When I used to run training meetings each week with clients, I would ask them, "How many people in the room have a license to drive?" Typically 100% of the hands go up. I then ask, "How many of you needed to take the driver's test more than once?" Inevitably 20-30% of the room raises their hands. And as such my point was made: "It makes no difference how many times it took. We all eventually master this skill."

"How many people here can ride a bicycle?" is the next question I ask. I go on to say, "Whether you learned the first day the training wheels came off or a week/month of almost countless tries, if you continued to arrest your fear and tried, you eventually mastered it."

I call this "The Bike Theory," in that when it comes to mastery of new skills, it makes no difference how often you fall off. How quickly you get back on determines the outcome of mastery, a pace that is always set by your ability to arrest your fears.

It is human nature for the emotion of fear to raise its limiting head as you try new things and encounter your comfort zones (defined by the mental crossroads of what you believe you are capable or not capable of). It cannot stop you unless you allow it to stop you.

The most successful salespeople I have ever studied reached their life's bounty through a state of mind they created of *how to be comfortable being uncomfortable.* This became a component of their overall mindset because they understood fear, welcomed it, and ultimately tamed it through consistent acts of courage—and, as such, the final component of the Swagger-Set.

Traits like courage, fearlessness, and risk tolerance all resonate from a mind rooted in the core belief that **your fear is your friend**.

A Force of One Hundred Thousand-Plus Souls

Over the past 30 years, my dedicated team and I at 2logical have directly and demonstrably impacted the success of countless souls by teaching them the "way of the sway," through the understanding and internalization of these five core beliefs. The emotional and documented results of these efforts have been memorialized in thousands of video and written testimonials throughout the years.

See Appendix A: Swagger Stories

Part III:

THE MASTER OF FUNDAMENTAL SELLING SKILLS: THE CALLING CARD OF ALL THOSE WHO SELL WITH SWAGGER

Chapter 7:

THE MASTER OF FUNDAMENTAL SALES SKILLS

"Sales professionals with Swagger are not adequate or average at the fundamental skills of their trade, they are lethal at them."

Under the strong leadership of my mentor, Randy, I and everyone this ninja hired was carefully and thoroughly trained on the fundamental selling skills in the classroom before we "took to the field"—meaning before we actually started speaking to live prospects.

As Randy put it, "My goal in the classroom is to help firmly seed the fundamental skills/techniques and strategies of the sales process you will need to become lethal in your sales career. However, it is in the field where the real rubber will meet the road…where the true growth and learning will take place." Boy, did I quickly come face to face with exactly what he meant.

My First Day in the Field

As we sat in the student center sipping coffee together and refining our game plan for the day (reviewing exactly which professors we were going to see and sell our new Macmillan Books), Randy calmly looked at me and said, "Joe, let me give you a clear picture of how we will work together today in the field."

"Okay," I said, bright eyed and chock full of enthusiasm.

"In the classroom," he went on, "we focused on identifying each stage of the sales process…what it is, how to execute it… and today we will be implementing what we have learned."

With not much more needed than the big positive smile on my face as acknowledgment, he went on. "How we are going to do this is, I am going to do the first sales call and you will observe. After each sales call, we will sit and ask ourselves together:

- What did I do right?
- What did I do wrong?
- What can I refine and do better on the next call that will make me more capable and powerful at getting the results we seek—a new sale?"

Again, I nodded in acknowledgment.

"Then you will do the next call, and again we will sit and reflect using these same three questions. We will follow this formula, taking turns throughout the day. Sound good?"

"I got it!" I exclaimed, and we gathered our belongings and headed to the faculty offices.

Upon arrival, we quickly found Professor Jacobs' office. Randy knocked, we were invited in, and I watched pure art in motion. It was amazing to watch this master of persuasion move. Executing with extreme enthusiasm, confidence and zeal, I watched Randy walk through each stage of the sales process, kneading and shaping the discussion down the exact path he taught in the classroom:

- Rapport
- Transitional Success Story
- Qualify
- Present
- Close
- Overcome Objections
- Referral/Network

Like a master chef, when the meeting was through, we had befriended Professor Jacobs and he agreed to give our new entry level chemistry book by Petrucci a try next semester.

"Wow," I thought, "the master chef sure does know how to make dough." I smiled as we walked over to a hall bench, where Randy asked me to sit so we could critique his sales interview.

"What did I do right, Joe? What did I do wrong? Most importantly, what can I do differently, adjust or refine to make my sales calls more capable of getting the result we seek—a new sale?"

As I sat, I wondered if this was a series of trick questions or perhaps a little joke. I had literally watched him do every single thing he taught in the classroom with extreme precision, grace, and most importantly, positive results. I thought carefully and finally said slowly, "Well, Randy, I think you followed the sales process to an exact 'T,' earning the right at each stage to go through the gate to the next stage…from rapport to the close right through to asking and getting referrals to other professors."

"Yes." He smiled confidently. And then he went on to review exactly what he did, why he did it and how the actions consummated the sale. "With the exception of one point in the conversation—with Professor Jacobs, I think I could have worded one of my questions in the qualify slightly differently. Otherwise, I think it went well."

He then exclaimed exuberantly, "You're up! Your turn. Dr. Jones, here we come!"

As I approached the office door, my palms began to sweat. "Can palms actually sweat?" I remember asking myself. I knocked on the door and politely asked Professor Jones if I could enter his office and perhaps speak with him about the upcoming semester's classes and what books he was considering using.

A little distracted but somewhat politely, Dr. Jones looked up and said, "Sure, gentlemen, come on in and have a seat. What can I do for you?"

"Welllll, Dr. Jjjjjjones…"

That was it! That was all I could muster up to say. I gulped in a big breath of air, blew it back out and proceeded to sweat from every single pore of my body. I never knew the human body could sweat like that—I remember thinking this as I disintegrated right before Dr. Jones'—and my boss Randy's—eyes.

Randy quickly recognized that I was done and swept in to save me, himself, and Dr. Jones from witnessing spontaneous human combustion right in front of them.

At the end of the meeting, Randy had expertly taken control, made a second sale, as I watched through cloudy eyes blinded by sweat. As we left Dr. Jones' office, I could not get out of that oven fast enough; I broke into a near-run as I shouted back to Randy, who was almost ten paces back, "Hurry up, Randy, we do not want to be late to our next call."

Randy had one hand up, trying to flag me down. He called out, "Joe, wait up. We need to talk."

"No," I called back, "we need to keep going. We do not want to be late!" I exclaimed.

"Joe!" he bellowed. "Stop. Sit down." He pointed sternly to a hall bench. "We need to talk. I have some questions for you."

"Yeah," I thought as I broke stride and headed for the bench. "I'll bet he is going to ask me what other careers I have considered, or something like that."

But instead, he simply caught his breath and said, "What did you do right? What did you do wrong? And what can you do differently, adjust or refine to make the next sales call more capable of getting the result we seek—a new sale?"

As I grappled for composure, I found myself quickly pondering all that I learned a few weeks ago in the sales training classroom, and all that I had just implemented—or didn't—with Dr. Jones. "Well, Randy, when I think about it in the context you have given me, it helps me to see that I really only did one thing right...I kept breathing!" I blurted out.

"Exactly!" he fired right back. He then went on to say, "I have never seen someone suck so much oxygen out of a room like that and blow it back in. It was amazing. In the next sales interview, I want you to work some words into it!"

The Jack-of-All-Trades, The Maser of None

Imagine dreaming of riches as an NBA star but never mastering the fundamental of dribbling the ball. Would you pay the price for a seat at an NBA game to watch players that could shoot but could not dribble, and others who could dribble like a champ but couldn't shoot to save their lives? I don't think so...there would be no Swagger, would there?

Muggsy Bogues, whom I mentioned earlier, could shoot, dribble, defend and even block shots—including one on 7' tall Patrick Ewing. What? You read that right. How the heck does that happen? Swagger!

Just as day cannot exist without night, Swagger cannot be achieved without complete and utter mastery of the fundamental skills of your trade. People will pay significant money to watch the very best play the magical game of hoops. Why? Swagger! People also pay significant money to those who master the fundamental selling skills/processes. Why? Swagger!

Recognizing the fundamental skills essential to sales is not nearly enough to Swagger-Sell. As Randy stated on our very first joint selling day, "It is the execution of these skills each and every day, with a critical eye fixated on improvement and mastery, that is where the rubber will meet the road."

Lack of Skill Mastery = Lack of Swagger

No one reaches the pinnacle of success in sports, the military, martial arts, personal finance, relationships, selling, or for that matter any role or aspect in life unless they understand, embrace and master the fundamental skills of their trade. We mentioned this briefly earlier.

One can no more become lethal in, say, basketball if they never master the fundamental skills of dribbling, shooting, running, defending, than they can become powerful at personal finances if they do not adopt, master and apply the ability to live below their means, save part of what they earn each month, and adhere to a save-and-then-buy strategy. Becoming the best in either of these examples or in anything you can think of requires complete and utter mastery of the fundamental skills and best practices (meaning application of these skills) in anything!

Those who learn to Swagger, first foster a different mindset—the Swagger-Set, which is comprised of five core governing beliefs. *It is the Swagger-Set that enables you to try, apply and ultimately master the fundamental selling skills needed to succeed!*

But why?

Swagger-Set Mastery + Skill-Set Mastery = Swagger!

As described in the first two parts of this book, those who master the ability to Swagger yield demonstrably stronger results in sales and in life than those who fail to walk life's path with this unique and powerful sway!

Together we have defined Swagger, best captured in the Urban Dictionary: "How one presents him or herself to the world. Swagger is shown from how a person handles a situation."

However, what has been most poignant in our journey up to now is that together we have isolated exactly what causes those who move with Swagger to act or react to life's situations (whether opportunities or challenges) differently is a distinct set of core governing beliefs that collectively we call the Swagger-Set.

Simply put, the Swagger-Set is the mindset comprised of five definitive core beliefs that I identified, tested, and went on to help tens of thousands of people use to master the fundamental skills and best practices needed to reach their full potential in sales and in life.

Throughout the years of my career, I have helped individual entrepreneurs start companies from scratch notes on a piece of paper, and then sell themselves with the help of their newfound business into countless millions of dollars in revenue—and yes, income, too.

By helping others discover and master the Swagger-Set needed for extreme sales success, my talented team of associates and I have helped countless individuals become the #1 sales talent in their company and in their respective industry: investments, pharmaceuticals, banking, insurance, real estate, energy, technology, and consumer and business products.

Old, young, tenured, new, male, female, and of all races and religions—none of these common demographics hindered their immediate and steadfast steps to the top. Their success was assured by the Swagger they personified in each and every step—meaning how they acted and/or reacted to:

- Each setback, challenge, roadblock they encountered
- Disappointment they endured from the underperformance or lack of commitment from those in key support roles on their team
- Distraction or environmental negative occurrences, such as adverse market conditions, product failures, fulfillment delays, and other obstacles.

And most importantly:

- Learning the fundamental sales skills they needed to master, and
- Execution of their sales plan

Application of the Swagger-Set: The Key to Sales Skill Mastery

So which came first, the chicken or the egg? I am not a philosopher or a scientist, but I do know from observation that all things throughout nature grow from the inside out. Trees grow in concentric circles from the inside out (you can see this when you cut a limb off of a trunk). Chickens grow from inside of a shell. You too grew from within your mother's womb.

As such, a Muggsy Bogues, an Abraham Lincoln, a Thomas Edison, a Boomer Esiason, a Jack Welch, an Elvis Presley, an Oprah Winfrey…we, like each of them, achieve mastery from the inside out. Muggsy had a Swagger-Set first, then spun his dream to play pro ball, by paying the dues of tireless study and practice of the fundamental skills of the game. My lifelong friend Boomer kicked off his life of Swagger with a dream and then studied, practiced and mastered the skills and strategies of the gridiron to reach the pinnacle of career success—and I watched it, participated in it on the paved streets of Long Island, NY, as he swayed his way.

No matter which icon you choose from above, it is the collection of thoughts and beliefs—a Swagger-Set—which is the enabler of skill mastery. As such, take a moment if you are new to the world of professional sales or if you are a tenured sales professional, and remember the core mental building blocks of Swagger, the five core beliefs placed in the Swagger Success Model below.

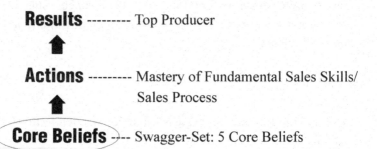

Results --------- Top Producer

↑

Actions --------- Mastery of Fundamental Sales Skills/
Sales Process

↑

Core Beliefs ---- Swagger-Set: 5 Core Beliefs

- **Power to Create:** If I cannot see myself, first, as the best, I cannot become the best. All success is created/ envisioned in my mind's eye first.

- **Unlimited Potential:** If I do not believe I can grow, change, adjust and "become," I will not persevere and work tirelessly to master the fundamental skills of my trade. We must believe we can before we will do the things we need to do.

- **Cause & Effect:** If I do not believe that all success is a function of cause and effect, I will focus on the wrong tasks and never consistently execute the right strategies (best practices) essential to my success. As such, I will fail to accept personal responsibility for my results (strong or weak).

- **Self-Efficacy/Self-Esteem:** I must see all feedback in life as not good or bad, but simply information to tap my potential. Otherwise, I will never persevere, remain positive and committed to skill mastery and achievement of my goals.

- **Fear is My Friend:** If I fail to recognize that fear is not my enemy but my friend, I will fail to dream, try new things, and execute on the ideas, plans and strategies needed to succeed.

Mastering Fundamental Selling Skills

In the remaining chapters, I have carefully laid out the core fundamental selling skills essential to sales success that, once mastered, will place you at the top of your sales organization. How do I know? I have consistently helped others just like you to do just that...after all, it is the only thing standing between you and your life dreams. Whether you are new or tenured in the profession of sales, each chapter will lay out 4 Swag-Steps that will expedite your path to skill mastery:

Swag-Step 1: The goal of this stage of the sales process
Swag-Step 2: The purpose/why of this stage
Swag-Step 3: The best practices/strategy
Swag-Step 4: The Swagger-Set Diagnostic Tool

Yes, you read Swag-Step 4 correctly; each chapter will help you apply the **Swagger-Set Diagnostic Tool** to help you reflect and quickly:

- Recognize what traits and beliefs are needed for the mastery of each fundamental selling skill if you are new to sales.
- Recognize what traits and beliefs may be lacking or not evolved to date if you are tenured (i.e. if you have more than two years of sales experience) and have yet to master a fundamental selling skill.

The path to Swagger is understanding that building and/or refining the right Mindset/Swagger-Set—the five Core Beliefs—is the first half of the formula. Why? Because without these proper beliefs, we lack the success traits essential to mastering the fundamental skills of our trade—the sales process.

The second half of our journey to Swagger Selling is to help you apply the Swagger-Set to ensure complete and utter mastery of the core fundamental sales skills essential to abundant sales success:

- Rapport
- Transitional Success Story
- Qualify
- Presentation
- Close
- Overcoming Objections
- Referral/Prospect/Network/Develop Centers of Influence

The next two pages illustrate what the tool looks like.

Swagger-Set Diagnostic Tool

Take a moment and reflect: Which trigger traits below best personify you…right now? Circle them.

Trigger Traits of Success	Trigger Traits of Failure
Swagger-Set (Optimal Core Beliefs)	No-Swagger (Limiting Beliefs)
Creative	Indifferent
Imaginative	Unimaginative
Positive	Negative
Persistent	Easily Discouraged
Resilient	Defeatist
Adaptive	Inability to Adapt/Change and Grow
Determined	Wavering
Courageous	Fearful
Confident	Lack of Confidence
Takes Initiative	Trapped by Inertia
Self-Reliant	Dependent
Self-Motivated	Lack of Motivation
Accept Personal Responsibility	Lack of Personal Responsibility
Abundant Mentality	Scarcity Mentality

Swag-Hint:

Remember—optimal or limiting—core beliefs yield trigger traits to success or failure that hide in plain sight.

Swagger-Set Diagnostic Tool

Which of these core beliefs best describes you? Circle all that apply.

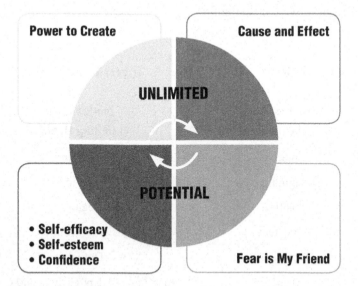

- **Power to Create:** If I cannot see myself, first, as the best, I cannot become the best. All success is created/envisioned in my mind's eye first.

- **Unlimited Potential:** If I do not believe I can grow, change, adjust and "become," I will not persevere and work tirelessly to master the fundamental skills of my trade. We must believe we can before we will do the things we need to do.

- **Cause & Effect:** If I do not believe that all success is a function of cause and effect, I will focus on the wrong tasks and never consistently execute the right strategies (best practices) essential to my success. As such, I will fail to accept personal responsibility for my results (strong or weak).

- **Self-Efficacy/Self-Esteem:** I must see all feedback in life as not good or bad, but simply information to tap my potential. Otherwise, I will never persevere, remain positive and committed to skill mastery and achievement of my goals.

- **Fear is My Friend:** If I fail to recognize that fear is not my enemy but my friend, I will fail to dream, try new things, and execute on the ideas, plans and strategies needed to succeed.

Chapter 8:

THE SECRET TO ESTABLISHING RAPPORT

"I Need You to Give Me Your Word!"

It was approximately thirty days since my first field training day with Randy when it finally happened. I was visiting the dean of the business department at Brockport College. I will not use the dean's name in case he is still top side of the grass, but it was an early solo sales call, the kind of encounter that could make or break the spirit and career of a newly minted sales professional.

It was early morning hours—I remember like it was yesterday. I knocked on the door and asked Dr. X if he had a few minutes for a chat. He invited me in, leaned back in his chair and curtly said, "What can I do for you?"

As I attempted my rapport-building skills—which at the time were grossly unevolved—he became agitated as I scanned the room looking for a common ground to talk about. As he leaned forward and pressed me to "skip the small talk," as he called it, I began to transition with a success story when all at once—and without saying a word—he pushed his chair back from his desk, walked over and opened his office door. He summoned me by taking his index finger and crinkling it up toward his palm.

I hesitated in shock and despair, and again—without saying a word—he pointed at me and then curled his index finger toward his palm again.

Stunned like an actor who has just forgotten his lines, I gathered my belongings and headed toward the door. As I closed the distance—which seemed like a mile rather than a mere ten feet—he himself stepped into the hallway so I could follow him out the door. When I finally passed the doorway and entered the hallway, he firmly stepped back into his office and slammed the door right in my face.

I stood there amidst my mixed state of raging emotions. I was not sure if I needed to scream, cry or quit. One second later I embraced all three in reverse order.

"I quit!" I said to myself. As I started to storm my way down the steps, out the door and toward my car, I began to cry (yes, I don't like admitting it to you or anyone, but I literally had tears of fear, anger, and defeat rolling down my cheek). That is, right until I got into my car. That's when the screaming began. "Who the hell does that man think he is? How dare he treat me like that? Who the hell would do this selling thing for a living? I must have been crazy to want to learn how to sell!"

And as I thrust into reverse out of my parking space and into drive with a churp in the wheels heading forward (which, by the way, is the reason why you never buy a used car that was part of a sales organization's fleet cars), I began thinking about exactly how I was going to call Randy and resign.

Still barreling down through the parking lot on my way to the main exit, screaming and ranting on…that's when it hit me. What hit me? It was a conversation Randy had with me—and I am guessing he had a similar conversation with everyone he recruited onto his team—on the day he on-boarded me.

"Joe, the financial and personal success that a man or a woman can reach in sales is boundless. However, I must warn you, in the early months it will not be easy. In fact, I need you to know that between résumé screening, phone screening and actual live interviews, I looked at more than 200 people before I found and hired you!

"I am not *hoping* you can succeed, I am not *wishing* you will succeed. I *know* you can do this and that you will be successful. But I must warn you, there will come a time or two in this first year that you are going to doubt yourself. There will come a time when every corpuscle in your body is going to tell you to quit. You must never quit! You must push on and through no matter what. Do you understand?"

"Yes," I remember saying as I wrapped my mind around this ominous prediction.

But it wasn't simply that memory that caused me to wipe my tears away and swiftly turn into the last parking slot just before the exit. It was what he said and did next.

"Good," he slowly responded when I said I understood. "I am glad you understand, because I need you to look me in the eyes and give me your word that you will not quit on yourself, your dreams and me when that moment comes. Do I have your word?"

"Yes, you have my word." That was the part in my memory that consumed my thoughts as I slowly put the car in park, collected my wares and headed back to the Brockport State business department—with a new goal, I might add: Sell more Macmillan business books into that department than any publishing sales representative had ever accomplished before, and befriend every single professor...

...Every one with the exception my nemesis, Dr. X, the leader of the business department—the person I viewed as the most responsible for helping all young rising adults succeed.

Swag-Step 1: The Goal of Rapport

The critical role that rapport plays for those who sell with Swagger is not to be underestimated. Although completing each stage of the sales process (Rapport, Transitional Success Story, Qualifying, Presenting, Closing, Overcoming Objections and Referral Prospecting) plays an integral role in making a sale, taking time to establish genuine rapport with every prospect lays the foundation needed to succeed at each of the remaining stages. This is because achieving success at each of the remaining stages of the sales process requires open communication between you and your prospect. Mastering the ability to establish rapport is the secret to establishing trust and to opening the lines of communication.

Swag-Step 2: The Purpose of Rapport

From a strategic standpoint, taking time to build rapport enables you to establish the proper emotional climate to conduct your sales interview. Although many salespeople erroneously believe that it is the prospect's responsibility to arrive at a sales interview upbeat, positive and ready to hear the sales message, in reality nothing could be further from the truth. It is important for you to recognize that it is your responsibility to ease the natural defenses of each prospect, thereby enabling you to open the lines of communication and create the proper emotional climate. This is best accomplished by devoting the first five to ten minutes of your sales interview to building genuine rapport with each prospect.

Understanding The Elements of Human Nature and Building Rapport

When attempting to build rapport, it is important to understand the powerful role the laws of human nature play in the communication between you and your prospect. Once you acknowledge the existence of these laws, you can consciously begin to use them to your advantage when meeting with a prospect for the first time.

I. The Defense Mechanisms of the Mind

It is a natural human instinct to be on guard when first meeting a total stranger. These protective instincts, which are present in both you and your prospect, typically create a state of mind that is tense and full of apprehension during the early stages of your sales interview. As a result, the ability to concentrate, listen and comprehend is, more often than not, a little off. These short circuits in the ability to communicate are the results of the natural defense mechanisms that the mind constructs to protect you and your image of "self." As a professional salesperson, not only must you acknowledge that these defense mechanisms exist in you and in your prospect, you must develop the ability to consciously disarm them through effective rapport building if you wish to become a Master of Sales and Swagger Sell your way to the top.

II. Human Emotions are Transferable

Have you ever walked into a room where people were having an intense and stressful conversation? You could almost cut the tension in the air with a knife. By simply being in the room, you too began to feel stressed. Have you ever been in a public place where a young child was inconsolable and crying profusely, and no matter how hard the parents try to comfort them, the child will not stop wailing? Within a moment, you become emotionally stressed, too.

These examples clearly demonstrate the highly contagious nature of human emotions. The simple fact is that any emotion that is truly dominant in a room or meeting is transferable—it will eclipse the emotional state of all who are present.

Those who sell with Swagger not only understand and acknowledge this fact, they accept personal responsibility to create strong rapport with each and every prospect they meet. How? Well, I can assure you they do not master this stage of the sales process by attempting to control other people's emotional state. They master it by recognizing that they must master their own emotions before and throughout each sales meeting, and by doing so—*really* doing so—they can and will transfer this same emotional state to their prospects.

Swag-Step 3: The Best Practices/Strategy for Building Rapport

Now that you understand how human nature influences your ability to build rapport, you can begin to apply proven techniques to disarm the defense mechanisms of the mind and establish the emotional climate of each sales meeting with Swagger precision.

I. Establishing a Genuine Common Ground

The fastest and easiest way to establish solid rapport with your prospect is to find a topic of common interest to discuss. Preferably, this topic should not be related to the business at hand. Following this strategy will enable you to relax the natural defenses that are present in both you and your prospect. Why? Because people relax faster and more thoroughly when they meet others that have similar interests, tastes and experiences.

When face-to-face with your prospect, you can usually find a topic of common interest to discuss by using creativity and personal observation. Look for pictures, memorabilia, a college ring or perhaps some unique art that you can discuss. In many cases, you will be calling on a lead that was generated through a referral. Asking the referent about the new prospect's personal interests or hobbies prior to the meeting will often enable you to quickly establish a common ground to build your rapport.

Even when teleselling (meaning conducting a sales interview over the phone), it is important to establish rapport by identifying a common ground with your prospect. This can be accomplished in a number of ways. You can Google the local news from the area you will be calling to get an update on local issues and events; contact the local Chamber of Commerce to get information about the city; find out if there are any major sporting events held in that part of the country or any other events of special interest. Following these strategies will significantly enhance your ability to build rapport. People, your prospects, will always become more relaxed and engaged on the phone with you if they see you have common things to talk about.

As a word of caution, when searching for a common ground, it is important to choose a topic of discussion that is of genuine interest to you. If you attempt to discuss a topic in which you do not have a sincere interest, your prospect will sense this and the walls of defense will strengthen and severely hamper your ability to communicate. Remember, only rapport that is built on a genuine common ground will enable you to: relax yourself and your prospect; gain control of the emotional climate of the interview; and thereby, deliver your sales message with the greatest probability of success through each of the remaining stages of the sales process.

II. Mirroring Modes of Communication

Did you ever notice the distinct differences in the way people communicate? Some people speak very slowly and methodically, while others speak very rapidly. Some people speak with a great deal of animation such as deep facial expressions, movement of their body. These vast differences are what keep life interesting. Nonetheless, as a professional salesperson, your ability to key in on these subtle differences is what enables you to communicate effectively with all different types of people.

Mirroring your prospect's mode of communication greatly enhances your ability to establish rapport. The reason this is such an effective tool is because human nature—once again—dictates that we are most relaxed and at ease when we are with people who remind us of ourselves. For example, if you speak very rapidly but your prospect speaks very slowly, it is important to adjust your speech pattern to their speed. If you are speaking with a person who uses a great deal of emotion and animation it is important to do the same.

A classic example of poor modeling is the fast-talking salesperson who attempts to sell a slow speaking prospect. What commonly happens in this situation is that a large portion of the sales message is missed by the prospect. As a result, the sale is often lost, not because the product or service was inappropriate, but because the prospect was not communicated in a mode that was appropriate for them. Even if the sale is made, the prospect often feels that they have been taken advantage of by a fast-talking salesperson. Even salespeople with the best intentions are sometimes viewed in a negative way because they have failed to master the essential skill of mirroring.

How do you know you have achieved genuine rapport?

As a professional sales trainer for more than thirty years, I have been asked by students countless times, "How will I know when I have achieved true rapport with the prospect?" I smile and reply, "You will know you have created earnest rapport when you yourself are truly relaxed and in a complete open and positive state of mind. Those with Swagger recognize that their dominant emotions are transferable."

A Summary of Swagger Fundamentals for Rapport

- The purpose of rapport is to ease the natural defenses of your prospect and open the lines of communication.
- Emotions are transferable; you, as the salesperson, set the emotional climate of each sales interview.
- Establish a genuine common ground with each new prospect.
- Mirror the speech pattern and body language of each new prospect.
- Rapport provides the emotional foundation needed for all subsequent stages of the sales process.

Swag-Step 4: The Swagger-Set Diagnostic Tool

The Power of Reflection

Only by truly establishing where you are now, can you crystallize your path forward to total sales mastery.

Identify your Trigger Traits

When it comes to your efforts so far to refine and master the fundamental and critical skill of rapport, which words best describe your behavior? (circle all that apply)

Trigger Traits of Success ⬆ Swagger-Set (Optimal Core Beliefs)	Trigger Traits of Failure ⬆ No-Swagger (Limiting Beliefs)
Creative	Indifferent
Imaginative	Unimaginative
Positive	Negative
Persistent	Easily Discouraged
Resilient	Defeatist
Adaptive	Inability to Adapt/Change and Grow
Determined	Wavering
Courageous	Fearful
Confident	Lack of Confidence
Takes Initiative	Trapped by Inertia
Self-Reliant	Dependent
Self-Motivated	Lack of Motivation
Accept Personal Responsibility	Lack of Personal Responsibility
Abundant Mentality	Scarcity Mentality

Identify your Core Beliefs

Circle which beliefs you know are helping you take the action needed to master this fundamental and critical skill: rapport.

Remember: Trigger Traits—for success or failure—are the outward reflection of your inner core beliefs.

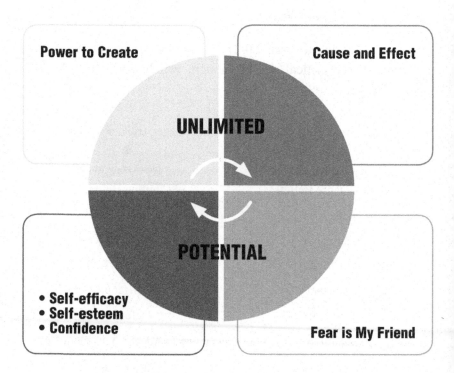

- **Power to Create:** If I cannot see myself, first, as the best, I cannot become the best. All success is created/ envisioned in my mind's eye first.

- **Unlimited Potential:** If I do not believe I can grow, change, adjust and "become," I will not persevere and work tirelessly to master the fundamental skills of my trade. We must believe we can before we will do the things we need to do.

- **Cause & Effect:** If I do not believe that all success is a function of cause and effect, I will focus on the wrong tasks and never consistently execute the right strategies (best practices) essential to my success. As such, I will fail to accept personal responsibility for my results (strong or weak).

- **Self-Efficacy/Self-Esteem:** I must see all feedback in life as not good or bad, but simply information to tap my potential. Otherwise, I will never persevere, remain positive and committed to skill mastery and achievement of my goals.

- **Fear is My Friend:** If I fail to recognize that fear is not my enemy but my friend, I will fail to dream, try new things, and execute on the ideas, plans and strategies needed to succeed.

Action Step: Reflect, Adjust, Succeed

Based upon your identified beliefs and traits, take a moment now to complete your reflection and determine your path forward with the exercise below.

When it comes to the fundamentals/Best Practices needed to master rapport:

I. What Have I Done Right?

II. What Have I Done Wrong?

III. What Will I Do Differently?

Chapter 9:

THE POWER OF A WELL ORGANIZED AND EXECUTED TRANSITIONAL SUCCESS STORY

"Too soon, too often, rather than too late and not enough."

It was exactly 32 business days before Randy flew back into town for our second work trip together in the field, doing what he and I both had a passion for—selling.

I was still very much a young colt, barely able to keep my feet under me, but it was no matter to the master of teaching Swagger, because upon taking the first sip of our coffee together in the student center on the college campus we were about to attack, he looked carefully into my eyes and said, "Today, Joe, we are going to slightly change-up what we did during our last work trip together. We will still take turns running each sales call and review them with our eyes fixed on constant refinement to the fundamental sales skills and best practices for each stage of the sales process. However, today we will focus each sales call only on one stage, and one stage only.

"Really?" I said with a puzzled look.

"Yes." He replied with exuberance, "We are going to pick a stage—like rapport—and we are going to not worry about using our time with the professor to qualify, present, close or anything else. I want you and I to see the tremendous depth a sales professional can take each skill and use it."

He went on, "It is not that we will not execute any of the other stages, but if we run out of time (we typically captured about 45 minutes with each professor), so be it.

"Let's start with rapport on this first call. I want you to see just how comfortable you can get and be with a total stranger by using the strategies you learned in class. I want you to really get to know who they are and for them to really get to know who you are. I want you to be in the moment and have fun with this. I will go first, then we will reflect:

- What did I do right?
- What did I do wrong?
- And most importantly, what will I adjust and refine so that I can be more powerful, more capable of getting the results we seek?"

Then you can take the next one. We will do this all day today and throughout the day tomorrow. Okay?" And without waiting for my response, he stood up and said, "Let's go, champ!"

These next two days (which flew by in the blink of an eye) were simply magical. They enabled me to practice extensively and with great detail each fundamental skill-set of the sales process. The practice, feedback (both negative, I assure you, and some positive) coupled with the safe environment he carefully created, was incredible. It was one more major step on the path to Swagger Selling (Mindset Mastery + Skill-Set Mastery = Swagger).

"Joe," Randy said as he got ready to board his flight home at the conclusions of our trip. "Those who become lethal in the world of sales and capture the abundance this career has to offer, do so because they master each stage of the sales process. They are not simply adequate at it, or just good at it—they practice it too soon, too often, rather than too late and not enough; until they are lethal at each and every stage of the sales process. Do you understand?"

"I absolutely do get it, and I will not let you or me down. I will not stop until I can do it as well as you can."

It sounds cocky as I reflect and write this, but it was not what I felt or meant. It was simply what I believed and was committed to doing. I saw the path to my skill mastery through the prism of my Swagger-Set. As such, I was fearless, driven, confident and determined to become the best.

"Great," he replied, and as he started to turn and head to the plane, he stopped—like a gear box that got caught—and said, "Remember, Joe, I believe in you."

For anyone committed to utter mastery of each stage of the sales process, the Transitional Success Story is a lethal ingredient of the formula. As a professional sales trainer, I have never seen, read or heard of this component to the sales process, ever. In fact, with myself and my gifted team of sales trainers, we have never seen this stage included and taught in any of the corporations that became our clients. It is nonexistent, and it is a huge misstep.

Why?

Simply put, it is a critical step to mentally lead the prospect out of the rapport stage and help them to now focus and engage in a hearty discussion about how your products and/or service solutions can potentially help them.

Swag-Step 1: The Goal of the Transitional Success Story

The Transitional Success Story accomplishes two critical things:

1. It breaks any preoccupation the prospect may have on their mind prior to your discussion.
2. It creates extreme credibility in the mind of the prospect.

The Transitional Success Story is not an introduction to your company. It is not a talk track filled with facts or figures or a product dump of what you have to offer. (I know you recognize that it is not the big dump, but you would be amazed how often I have witnessed new and seasoned salespeople just unload in the first five minutes of a sales call.)

The Transitional Success Story is a strategically guided mental missile, designed to vaporize any distractions and immediately get your prospect to lean in mentally to your conversation.

Swag-Step 2: The Purpose of the Transitional Success Story: Human Nature and the Power of a Success Story

Since we were all young children, we loved and relished the time of day we all know as "story time." Perhaps this was bedtime for you when your parents read you a book, or in kindergarten when the teacher read the class a story, or family dinners where the day's experiences are often shared. We are all conditioned to mentally stop—even if we do not want to—when someone begins to tell us a story.

In addition, the yearning of the human soul is to grow, become, succeed. As such, we are all immediately mentally drawn and attracted to successful people and things.

A carefully crafted, well thought through and perfected story of you and your company helping a past or current client solve a problem, overcome an obstacle and/or achieve a desirable result is the key to the Transitional Success Story.

> *"Dr. Smith, thank you for your time today. I have been truly looking forward to visiting with you. Are you familiar with Macmillan Publishing Textbooks?*
>
> *"Well, that is of little surprise. Because many of the professors I visit with have not had the opportunity to capture the attention and imagination of their students with Macmillan's incredible textbooks. This is especially true among the chemistry professors where until just recently, Macmillan did not have much to offer. That all changed with several of the blockbuster books they released this past fall that have been adopted at the University of Rochester, Buffalo, and Syracuse, to name a few. And they have been embraced overwhelmingly by faculty and students alike, because of the strategic editorial process of author selection and textbook development from which all Macmillan textbooks are created.*
>
> *"The institutions I mentioned harbor among the very best medical, scientific and engineering curricula, coupled with the best student talent in the world. Each have adopted these books,*

and have seen how these new teaching tools have helped students commit, persist and succeed in core classes that have been a huge challenge to them and the professors in the past.

"This is a brief collage of letters from faculty and students expressing this profound positive impact...

"It is pretty exciting, Dr. Jones, isn't it? But enough about Macmillan and our wares, so to speak—I am interested in finding out what classes you are teaching this year, and learning about the books and tools you have been using, and seeing if my firm and I can be of any help. Dr. Jones, what classes will you be teaching this year?"

In the word track above, you can see and feel the magnetic power of the Transitional Success Story. No matter what your company's product or services, you can and must break any mental preoccupation your prospect may have and capture their attention regarding the potential business at hand by crafting and perfecting your <u>Transitional Success Story</u>.

Swag-Step 3: Proven Techniques for Building Your Transitional Success Story

The questions below will help guide you in how to construct your Transitional Success Story.

1. What is it that you and your company truly have to offer to your clients/prospects?
   - What problems do you solve?
   - What opportunities do you help them to better capture?
2. What, if any, is your company's unique differential advantage over the competition?
   - Does an actual advantage exist?
   - If one does not exist (a more common dilemma than you may realize), what is the way you and your organization create a differential advantage in the mind of the customer?

3. Isolate a happy and fulfilled client who uses your products(s) and/or service(s) and is ecstatic. We all have these clients in our book of business.
   - Isolate: Why are they so happy?
   - What problem did you help them overcome?
   - What opportunity did you help them capture?

Reviewing and answering these few questions above will enable you to see how to organize and tell your success story to each prospect, capture their imagination regarding what is possible, and speak to their soul regarding the potential of your ability to help them succeed—all from the encounter they are about to have with you today.

The Transitional Success Story is one of the most overlooked steps of the sales process...and overlooking it is a deadly mistake. Take time, right now, to develop or refine your Transitional Success Story. Commit it to memory by practicing it until you can share it with extreme enthusiasm and focus, and watch the impact it has on each and every sales call you conduct for the rest of your career.

A Summary of Swagger Fundamentals for the Transitional Success Story

- The goal of the Transitional Success Story is to capture the prospect's attention regarding the potential business at hand.
- A powerful Transitional Success Story breaks the preoccupation that may exist in the prospect's mind prior to your discussion, creates extreme credibility and builds enthusiasm for your product/service.
- The Transitional Success Story illustrates your ability to potentially help the prospect solve a problem and/or capture an opportunity.
- Establish your product's/service's unique differential advantage.
- Everyone is attracted to success; always build curiosity and capture interest with a powerful client success story.

Swag-Step 4: The Swagger-Set Diagnostic Tool

The Power of Reflection

Only by truly establishing where you are now, can you crystallize your path forward to total sales mastery.

Identify your Trigger Traits

When it comes to your efforts so far to refine and master the fundamental and critical skill of the Transitional Success Story, which words best describe your behavior? (circle all that apply)

Trigger Traits of Success ⬆ Swagger-Set (Optimal Core Beliefs)	Trigger Traits of Failure ⬆ No-Swagger (Limiting Beliefs)
Creative	Indifferent
Imaginative	Unimaginative
Positive	Negative
Persistent	Easily Discouraged
Resilient	Defeatist
Adaptive	Inability to Adapt/Change and Grow
Determined	Wavering
Courageous	Fearful
Confident	Lack of Confidence
Takes Initiative	Trapped by Inertia
Self-Reliant	Dependent
Self-Motivated	Lack of Motivation
Accept Personal Responsibility	Lack of Personal Responsibility
Abundant Mentality	Scarcity Mentality

Identify your Core Beliefs

Circle which beliefs you know are helping you take the action needed to master this fundamental and critical skill: the Transitional Success Story.

Remember: Trigger Traits—for success or failure—are the outward reflection of your inner core beliefs.

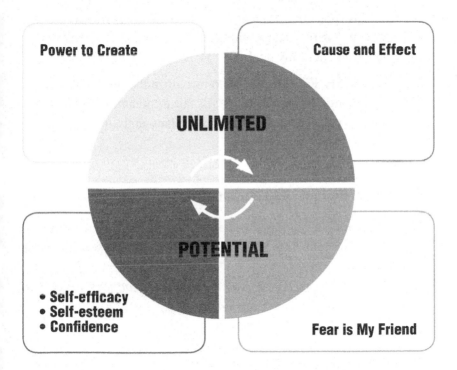

- **Power to Create:** If I cannot see myself, first, as the best, I cannot become the best. All success is created/ envisioned in my mind's eye first.

- **Unlimited Potential:** If I do not believe I can grow, change, adjust and "become," I will not persevere and work tirelessly to master the fundamental skills of my trade. We must believe we can before we will do the things we need to do.

- **Cause & Effect:** If I do not believe that all success is a function of cause and effect, I will focus on the wrong tasks and never consistently execute the right strategies (best practices) essential to my success. As such, I will fail to accept personal responsibility for my results (strong or weak).

- **Self-Efficacy/Self-Esteem:** I must see all feedback in life as not good or bad, but simply information to tap my potential. Otherwise, I will never persevere, remain positive and committed to skill mastery and achievement of my goals.

- **Fear is My Friend:** If I fail to recognize that fear is not my enemy but my friend, I will fail to dream, try new things, and execute on the ideas, plans and strategies needed to succeed.

Action Step: Reflect, Adjust, Succeed

Based upon your identified beliefs and traits, take a moment now to complete your reflection and determine your path forward with the exercise below.

When it comes to the fundamentals/Best Practices needed to master the Transitional Success Story:

I. What Have I Done Right?

II. What Have I Done Wrong?

Ill. What Will I Do Differently?

Chapter 10:

THE KEY TO CONSULTATIVE SELLING: BECOMING A MASTER QUALIFIER

> *"Prospects care very little about how much you know until they first see how much you care."*

It was a winter morning and Randy had just flown into Buffalo for our next adventure together in the field—selling.

"Cold one today," I said as we parked the car and headed for the student center for our preplanning and, of course, a hot cup of coffee.

"It is always cold in Buffalo, Joe. I think the only time it is not freezing here is during the two weeks of summer you get in early July," he quipped back.

Funny, still to this day—30-plus years later—we banter back and forth about the brutal winter weather we get in upstate New York; always rubbing it in my face about the sun and warmth of San Francisco, California. He always fails to mention the earthquakes.

As we shook off the cold, savored our hot coffee and began to review the game plan for the day, Randy seized the moment to sharpen both my mindset and skill-set with a simple question.

"Joe, it has been six months now that you have been in the field selling. I am curious. What do you think is the most important selling skill of all of the stages in the sales process?"

I smiled on the inside (have you ever done that?) because I knew the answer. "Closing," I said. "The best salespeople are the best closers."

"Why do you think it's the closing stage?"

I pondered for a moment and said, "Because it is the hardest part. It's the hardest part because you have to have the courage to ask for the order and the discipline to keep closing when they do not buy."

He looked at me with a larger-than-life smile and asked, "Tell me about your most recent sale of Petrucci's introduction to chemistry book. Why did they adopt it?" (Sales are called adoptions in the college publishing industry.)

I reflected for a moment. "Well, they adopted it primarily to help address a problem the students were having regarding stoichiometry"—a fancy word for mathematics. "That was the biggest reason. Petrucci covered stoichiometry earlier in the book than the textbook they were using, and the professor liked this because it gave him and the students more time throughout the semester to teach and learn it."

"How did you find out this critical piece of information?"

"I asked him questions when I first interviewed him," I said.

"And has it worked for them?" he asked slowly.

I said, "Hell, yeah. The professor loves it and so do his students. In fact, several other professors in the department are going to adopt it this fall."

"Joe," he tapped on in my brain (I hated when he did that and he did it all the time). "Why did Professor Johnson adopt the book?"

I paused for a moment, and then said, "Because I helped him…I helped him to see how the Petrucci book could solve his problem and substantially help his students."

"So did he adopt the book primarily because you closed him, or did he adopt the book because you helped him?"

The light was dawning now. "Because I was able to help him," I responded slowly.

Randy smiled. "That is correct. And how did you know how to best help him?"

"I asked him questions."

"Exactly!" He leaned back with the look of pride that a father or mother gets when their child finally learns how to walk.

He then wrapped up with a simple but profound statement that left an indelible impression in my mind forevermore. "Joe, prospects care very little about how much you know until they recognize how much you care about their challenges, their opportunities and their goals." He continued, "The masters of sales are people that are truly committed to *helping* each prospect they sit with, not *selling* the people they sit with; and the only way to truly help them is to become lethal at asking questions (Qualifying). However, not just any questions—you need to ask the right questions in the right order that creates clarity of thought in each prospect's mind."

And with that mental grenade firmly planted in my head, he gulped down the last drop of warmth from his coffee, leaped up and said, "Time to go make rain...or shall I say, hail. Ha, ha, ha!"

Swag-Step 1: The Goal of Qualifying

Simply put, the goal of the qualify is to crystallize the answers to the following questions, both in your mind's eye and in the mind of your prospect: *Where* are they now, *where* do they want to go, *when* do they want to get there, and *what* will it mean to them to get there— meaning why is it important to them.

The ability to thoroughly qualify a prospect is the most challenging, yet most rewarding aspect of the sales process. This stage is challenging because it requires the professional salesperson to ask probing, strategic questions and to listen intently to the responses. However, the benefits salespeople gain by mastering the ability to effectively qualify a prospect far outweigh the effort it takes to be thorough, to face their fear, and to step through their comfort zones to ask the tough questions.

Benefits of Becoming a Master Qualifier

- Strategically positions the salesperson as an expert
- Isolates key buying motives and creates urgency to buy
- Shortens buying cycle by assuring the salesperson is in front of key decision makers
- Clarifies hot buttons and, thereby, makes for significantly stronger product presentations/recommendations
- Helps salesperson uncover needs that might otherwise go unnoticed (which improves cross-sell ratio)
- Removes objections and sales stalls before they happen
- Dramatically improves closing ratio
- Lays the groundwork for getting referrals
- Most importantly, it is the key to helping your prospect see how much you care and are committed to helping them get what they want

Product Selling vs. Consultative Selling

In the mind of each prospect and in the unwritten ethical bylaws of sales, there is a marked difference between product selling (e.g. non-professional selling) and consultative selling (e.g. professional selling), and those with Swagger recognize the clear difference between the two.

The product salesperson focuses only on pushing their product or service, giving little to no attention to the true overriding needs and wants of the prospect. In fact, in many cases the non-professional salesperson will not even take the time to isolate the wants and needs of their prospect. Rather, they will make an assumption regarding what the prospect needs and immediately launch into their "sales pitch," attempting to convince them to buy. The classic extreme example of the non-professional salesperson is the roadside "used car" salesperson who takes one look at you and says, "Boy, do I have the perfect car for you..."

Conversely, the true professional consultative salesperson lives by the Universal Law of Reciprocation (also known as the Law of Service), which states: "The only way to get what I want out of life is to help enough other people get what they want out of life." This powerful philosophy has dramatic ramifications in the sales arena. By shifting each sales call from making assumptions and blind product pitches to asking a series of strategic questions to clarify needs, wants and isolate challenges, and then making a product or service recommendation that directly addresses the exact needs/wants/challenges, you become an invaluable resource to each and every prospect.

Never forget, a comprehensive qualify psychologically communicates to each prospect a loud and clear message: "I truly care about you. I am a professional. I am here to help you identify, isolate and solve problems, and I am sincerely interested in addressing your specific needs." Bottom line, mastering the ability to qualify positions you as a powerful consultant, an expert who helps clients consistently, solves challenges, improves situations and captures new opportunities.

Swag-Step 2: The Purpose of Qualifying: "Create Clarity of Thought in the Mind of Your Prospect."

When you consider that most prospects spend their days in the heat of the battle, juggling a multitude of tasks, it is easy to see how challenging it can be for them to always have an objective view of what is truly happening around them. As a result, most prospects you will sit down with will be adept at articulating problems, yet woefully deficient at identifying solutions to those challenges. In your role as the professional salesperson, you have the ability to apply your specialized knowledge (i.e. your product and industry expertise) with an objective viewpoint. This perspective will, many times, allow you to find solutions that a prospect would never come to without your assistance.

However, just because you have the ability to clearly see how your product/service will provide a solution does not automatically mean a prospect will buy. Why? In the world of professional selling there is an old axiom that states, "A confused mind is not a buying mind." Many times, through their own confusion, a prospect cannot see what, to you, is black and white.

Mastering your ability to strategically sequence your qualifying questions to create clarity in your mind and in your prospect's thought process is the very crux of the "power of persuasion." Ultimately, a proper qualify creates a clear divide or chasm between "where the prospect is now" and "where they would like to be in the future." Once created, this chasm provides two perfect anchoring points for you to bridge the divide with your product or service.

Swag-Hint

A perfect qualify provides solid anchoring points for you to bridge the gap between where a prospect is now and where they want to be in the future.

Swag-Step 3: The Best Practices/Strategy of Qualifying

Regardless of product or service, master salespeople follow the same qualifying best practices/strategies with each prospect. This strategy revolves around isolating four key elements: Where is the prospect right now? Where does the prospect want to be in the future? What has stopped them from getting there already? And lastly, why is it important to them to get there? Let's take a moment and explore the strategy behind each of these critical steps of the qualify.

1. Isolating Exactly Where They Are Now

The first step in effectively qualifying a prospect's true wants and needs is to always establish a solid foundation to build your sales recommendation upon. Isolating where the prospect is "now" creates the critical foundation from which all buying decisions will be made. Therefore, you will want to focus your questions exclusively on issues that pertain to the current status quo.

Swag-Hint

Remember, the essential goal of a good qualify is to take a confused mind and make the thought process clear. By carefully and strategically establishing a division between your "now" oriented questions and your "future" oriented questions, you help each prospect to crystallize the wants and needs required to make a buying decision.

For example, some "now" oriented questions for an office equipment salesperson may be:

- *What equipment are you currently working with?*
- *Why did you select this equipment when you originally purchased it?*

- *What do you like about your current equipment?*
- *What do you dislike?*
- *Other than what you have mentioned, are there any other challenges that you are currently facing with regard to...?*
- *In addition to yourself, who else will be involved in making this decision?*

On the following page is an Action Step that will assist you in developing the appropriate 'Where are they now?" qualifying questions for your product or service.

Swag-Hint

Establishing where your prospect is "Now" creates the first foundational anchoring point for your possible recommendation(s).

Action Step

Take a moment and develop a series of "Where are you now" type questions. Be sure to ask for all relevant information you need to collect.

1.

2.

3.

4.

5.

6.

7.

8.

9.

10.

Swag-Hint

At times (although not always), the product/service you are selling has a distinct differential advantage over the competition (like Petrucci covering the mathematics of chemistry—stoichiometry—early in the semester). If a differential exists, you will want to probe to see if you can establish a need/want for this in the qualify to help shape the chasm you are creating.

2. Isolating Exactly Where They Want to Be in the Future

Once you have defined in both your mind and the prospect's mind exactly where they are now, you will want to transition to questions relating to where they would like to be in the future. Remember, by strategically dividing your "Now" and "Future" questions, you are able to create a clear divide or "chasm" in the mind of your prospect. This chasm establishes the need/wants and creates discomfort or discontentment with maintaining the status quo. Some sample "Future" oriented questions might be:

- *You mentioned that your current solution (service/product being used) offers X, Y and Z; what do you wish it offered that it currently does not?*
- *If you could craft the ideal service/product solution to help you accomplish _____, what would you want it to look like?*
- *With regard to _____, if you could design/redesign _____ to exactly meet your needs, how would it be structured?*
- *What would you like to see happen with your _____ over the next 12-24 months?*

On the following page is an Action Step that will assist you in developing the appropriate "future" oriented qualifying questions for your product or service.

Swag-Hint

Establishing where your prospect wants to be in the "Future" creates the second foundational anchoring point for your product/service recommendation.

Action Step

Take a moment and develop a series of "future" oriented questions. If possible, be sure to include future questions that isolate or create a differential advantage regarding your service/product solution.

1.

2.

3.

4.

5.

6.

7.

8.

9.

Swag-Hint

Remember, the essential goal of a good qualify is to take a confused mind and make the thought process clear. By carefully and strategically establishing a division between your "now" oriented questions and your "future" oriented questions, you help each prospect to crystallize in their mind the wants and needs required to make a buying decision.

3. Isolating Both the Tangible and Intangible Barriers that Have Prevented Your Prospect From Bridging the Chasm In the Past

Once you have defined both sides of your sales chasm (i.e. where they are now and where they want to go), the next critical step to helping your prospect is to isolate the issues that have stopped them from arriving at that "future" point already. A few ways to phrase this powerful question:

1. "If this is what you want/need, what are the things that have prevented it from happening in the past?" (Tangibles: Budget, time, goals/plan, etc. Intangibles: Fear of failure, inertia, procrastination, political risk, etc.)
2. "If this is what you want/need, why don't you have it now? What has gotten in the way?"

Often, this line of questioning begins to demonstrate the point that procrastination has been a significant deterrent to accomplishing what the prospect truly wants. Given this response, you now have a powerful means to thwart the natural human resistance to following through with the inevitable decision to purchase.

Swag-Hint

As you will see in the upcoming chapter on closing, many times in closing the sale, prospects will use common stalls such as, "I'm just not sure this is the right time," "Why don't you call me back next week," "I need to think about it," or something of a similar nature. By taking a consultative approach, conducting a proper qualify and isolating what has stopped them in the past, you now have both the right and the ability to respond with, "Jerry, you shared with me that the biggest thing that has stopped you from getting where you truly want and need to be is procrastination. By moving on this now, you'll be accomplishing those things which you shared were truly important to …."

Action Step

Take a moment and craft a question or two that you can begin using tomorrow to help your prospect see exactly what has stopped them in the past.

1.

2.

4. Why Is It Important to the Prospect to Take Action? (Isolating the Emotional Buying Motive)

It is a well-known fact that human beings make the majority of their decisions based on emotion. While many people will vehemently argue that all of their decisions are based on sound logic, in reality, we all make emotional decisions and then attempt to justify them logically. Since most purchasing decisions are made based on emotional "wants" rather than logical "needs," failure to identify both aspects of your prospect's motives to purchase is a cardinal mistake. The reason for this is because unlike logical needs, the emotional wants for a product/service can differ drastically from one prospect to another. It is essential never to assume you know the prospect's emotional wants.

The first three steps in the Consultative Qualifying Process are designed to define your prospect's logical needs and create a logical chasm between the prospect's current situation and where they truly would like to be. However, we realize that people do not make decisions based solely upon logic. So, how does a professional salesperson turn a logical chasm into an emotional one? They make this critical transition with one simple three-letter word: **Why?** Why is it a personal benefit to them to put your solution in place, today?

Sample Why Questions:

- *[NAME], what will it mean to your organization to have this (equipment/service/solution) in place?*
- *What will it mean to you personally to solve this challenge once and for all?*

Swag-Hint

Always remember, if you are having a problem with closing, it can most often be traced back to a problem in qualifying. The reason is simple: If you have done a thorough qualify, followed by an adequate presentation, the close becomes the natural ending to an orderly progression. Why? Because sales outcomes, just like all things in life, are the result of cause and effect. The sales process we are studying and committed to mastering is based on cause and effect.

Action Step

Take a moment and write out two ways you can begin creating the emotional charge/energy needed to motivate your prospect to act:

1.

2.

5. Creating Urgency (When Needed)

At times, a prospect will attempt to stall (in the closing stage) by postponing the need to make a decision to follow your recommendation to buy. This late stage stall can be dramatically reduced by asking one last question in the qualifying stage of your sales interview:

"[NAME], when would you ideally like to see this (these) challenges/opportunities that we have been discussing resolved/captured?"

This question is typically answered with comments like, "Now," or "Yesterday." As such, it creates the urgency you want and need for the upcoming closing stage you are sequencing to.

The 7 Most Common Mistakes Salespeople Make in Qualifying

To those committed to selling with Swagger, the qualify is the most important aspect of successfully completing any sales call. Qualifying also is the aspect of the sales process that requires the highest degree of skill. As a result, it is common for salespeople to make fundamental mistakes in the qualify that short-circuit the sales process in later stages. This list, comprised of the seven most common mistakes salespeople make, will help raise your awareness so that you will be able to avoid them.

Common Qualifying Mistake #1: No Chasm—No Close

Countless salespeople compromise their position by allowing a prospect to prompt them into making a presentation of their product/service without completing a thorough qualify. Never hesitate to end a sales interview with a prospect if you are unable to accomplish a thorough qualify.

Remember, the key to being a professional salesperson and selling with Swagger is rooted in your ability to help people get what they want, not to manipulate or force them to buy a product or service they do not want and really do not need. By personally committing to conduct a sales presentation only after you have thoroughly qualified a prospect, you immediately differentiate yourself from the rest of the thundering herd of salespeople in your industry. Your commitment to qualifying will give you an almost magical power with every prospect you meet. Each prospect will immediately sense your commitment and heightened level of professionalism, as well as your deep concern and desire to help them. As a result, your prospect will be more open and allow you to help them.

In summary, never allow a prospect to push you into a sales presentation before thoroughly qualifying them. As you continue to anchor yourself to the basics of professional consultative selling, you will find the purpose of terminating a sales interview that is not progressing effectively, is not only acceptable, it is essential.

Although one would not want to make a habit of walking out on sales interviews, at times it is necessary to politely end a sales interview when you are unable to thoroughly qualify the prospect. In those select rare occasions that you are forced to take this course of action, you will realize that your esteem and confidence in yourself and our profession of sales demonstrably appreciate in value. Those who move each day with Swagger move with conviction about who they are, what they do and how they do it!

Common Qualifying Mistake #2: Using Your Ears and Your Mouth Disproportionately

"Selling is not telling; it is listening." We have each been gifted with two ears and one mouth and the professional salesperson uses them proportionately. Your ability to close sales is dependent upon your skill to sequentially ask sound qualifying questions and effectively listen to the prospect's replies. Only when you shut everything out of your mind and focus on the chosen words, emotions and body language of the person with whom you are communicating, can you truly capture their thoughts and needs. Since very few people ever truly master this level of listening, you stand out with each prospect with whom you interact. Your listening reinforces that you truly care.

Since your ability to deliver an effective sales presentation is dependent upon tuning into the needs/emotions/wants of your prospect, you must constantly strive to heighten your ability to listen if you wish to become a top producing salesperson and a master of Swagger.

Common Qualifying Mistake #3: Asking Random Questions

Many times, new or inexperienced salespeople will approach the qualifying stage of a sales interview with no true strategy in mind. This random approach, more often than not, results in the salesperson asking a series of unrelated, random questions that, at best, takes a confused mind and makes it more confused. Rest assured, this is not a good thing if the goal is to make a sale. However, many salespeople hope that taking this random, shotgun approach to qualifying will elicit some response with a sliver of a need or desire to purchase. With this sliver in hand, the non-professional salesperson mistakenly feels they have what they need to conduct a sales presentation.

Remember that the true purpose of conducting a consultative qualify is to create clarity of thinking in the mind of your prospect. This clarity only comes from creating a true chasm between where your prospect is now and where she ultimately desires to be. Random questions only serve to cloud the thought process of your prospect; a cardinal mistake that those with Swagger never make.

Common Qualifying Mistake #4: Not Selling to the "Right" Person

Countless hours are wasted in the business of sales selling to people who are not in the position to make a buying decision. Knowing this, the professional salesperson will always take the time early in the qualify to ask the question, "In addition to yourself, who else is involved in the purchasing decision?" A prospect's response to this question very quickly isolates all the decision makers. With this information in hand, the professional salesperson is able to determine if they should focus the balance of the sales call on closing for the order or closing to get an appointment with the true decision makers.

One other important point to note with regard to selling to the right person: notice how the question above is phrased, "In addition to yourself, who else is involved in the purchasing decision?" If the individual is not the ultimate decision maker, asking the question in this manner takes them out of the corner, empowers them and increases the likelihood that they will help you to get in front of the right people. Those who sell with Swagger are masters of making sure they sit and sell to true decision makers.

Common Qualifying Mistake #5: Assuming

The vast majority of sales are lost because a salesperson did not adequately qualify out the true wants, needs and emotional drivers of their prospect. In this scenario, more often than not, the critical qualifying stage is skipped altogether or given too little emphasis, which in turn forces the salesperson to make broad assumptions as to what the prospect wants and needs. In many cases, making these assumptions causes the salesperson to place too much emphasis on things that are not important to the prospect and too little emphasis on things that are important.

Qualifying with Swagger defines logical and emotional hot buttons, creates discomfort with maintaining the status quo (i.e. urgency to buy) and positions the salesperson as an expert resource who can help resolve challenges. Never assume!

Common Qualifying Mistake #6: Selling Logically

For those salespeople who have taken the time to develop their qualifying skills, the most common mistake is to not define "Why" it is important to the prospect to make a purchasing decision. Remember, people make emotionally motivated decisions, which they then attempt to justify with logic.

The responses that a prospect gives with regard to where they are now and where they would like to be are logical in nature. Asking these types of questions, therefore, creates a logical chasm that will help the prospect justify his decision to buy. However, without some type of emotional charge/desire to take action, many times a decision will not be made. Asking "Why" creates the emotional desire.

All those who sell with Swagger recognize the need to conjure emotion, and that it is impossible to answer the "Why" question logically.

Common Qualifying Mistake #7: Ending the Qualify Too Soon

Successfully qualifying a prospect's wants and needs requires patience, strategy and poise. It requires strategy in the form of knowing when and in what order to ask questions. Qualifying requires patience because a salesperson with Swagger will never pounce on the first buying signal that a prospect provides. Rather, they will take the time to gather all of the relevant information and then, and only then, will they make their comprehensive service/product recommendation.

Too often in the qualifying stage, salespeople will see a singular need for their product or service and will immediately leave the qualifying stage and launch into a sales recommendation. While this at times may result in a sale, in most cases it results in missed opportunities for additional sales. Being patient and completing a full qualify provides a salesperson with all of the information they need to effectively make a comprehensive product recommendation, which frequently results in higher sales volume. Those with Swagger always sell with patience, strategy and poise.

A Summary of Swagger Fundamentals for Qualifying

- The goal of qualifying is to create clarity of thought in the mind of each prospect.
- A strategic qualify creates a chasm between where the prospect is now, and where the prospect wants to go.
- Crystallize where the prospect is now (ask questions that pertain to the current situation/status).
- Crystallize where the prospect wants to be in the future (ask questions that pertain to their ideal future).
- Isolate the tangible and intangible barriers that have prevented your prospect from bridging this chasm in the past (ask questions like, "If this is what you want/need, why don't you have it now?").
- Isolate the emotional buying motive (ask questions that pertain to "why" this is important to the prospect).
- Create urgency, when needed (ask questions that pertain to "when" they would like to see change; a new result).

Swag-Step 4: The Swagger-Set Diagnostic Tool

The Power of Reflection

Only by truly establishing where you are now, can you crystallize your path forward to total sales mastery.

Identify your Trigger Traits

When it comes to your efforts so far to refine and master the fundamental and critical skill of qualifying, which words best describe your behavior? (circle all that apply)

Trigger Traits of Success ⬆ Swagger-Set (Optimal Core Beliefs)	Trigger Traits of Failure ⬆ No-Swagger (Limiting Beliefs)
Creative	Indifferent
Imaginative	Unimaginative
Positive	Negative
Persistent	Easily Discouraged
Resilient	Defeatist
Adaptive	Inability to Adapt/Change and Grow
Determined	Wavering
Courageous	Fearful
Confident	Lack of Confidence
Takes Initiative	Trapped by Inertia
Self-Reliant	Dependent
Self-Motivated	Lack of Motivation
Accept Personal Responsibility	Lack of Personal Responsibility
Abundant Mentality	Scarcity Mentality

Identify your Core Beliefs

Circle which beliefs you know are helping you take the action needed to master this fundamental and critical skill: qualifying.

Remember: Trigger Traits—for success or failure—are the outward reflection of your inner core beliefs.

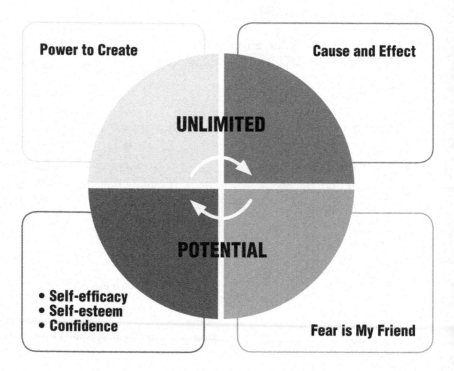

- **Power to Create:** If I cannot see myself, first, as the best, I cannot become the best. All success is created/ envisioned in my mind's eye first.

- **Unlimited Potential:** If I do not believe I can grow, change, adjust and "become," I will not persevere and work tirelessly to master the fundamental skills of my trade. We must believe we can before we will do the things we need to do.

- **Cause & Effect:** If I do not believe that all success is a function of cause and effect, I will focus on the wrong tasks and never consistently execute the right strategies (best practices) essential to my success. As such, I will fail to accept personal responsibility for my results (strong or weak).

- **Self-Efficacy/Self-Esteem:** I must see all feedback in life as not good or bad, but simply information to tap my potential. Otherwise, I will never persevere, remain positive and committed to skill mastery and achievement of my goals.

- **Fear is My Friend:** If I fail to recognize that fear is not my enemy but my friend, I will fail to dream, try new things, and execute on the ideas, plans and strategies needed to succeed.

Action Step: Reflect, Adjust, Succeed

Based upon your identified beliefs and traits, take a moment now to complete your reflection and determine your path forward with the exercise below.

When it comes to the fundamentals/Best Practices needed to master qualifying:

I. What Have I Done Right?

II. What Have I Done Wrong?

III. What Will I Do Differently?

Chapter 11:

CREATING A STRATEGIC SALES PRESENTATION
(THE FIRST HALF OF THE SALES PROCESS)

"The world meets no one halfway."

Back from the Future...One day on vacation with Michelle (my better half) and my three sons, I watched an amazing feat by an entertainer at Sea World in Orlando, Florida. There was a clown on roller skates, skating backwards and juggling three bowling pins with his hands. That was astonishing enough, but what was even more amazing was that the clown was also juggling three ping pong balls with his mouth, by catching them on his lips and blowing them back into the air...all the while juggling these bowling pins with his hands and roller skating backwards.

This clown had Swagger! Why? He possessed extreme skill!

Have you ever actually seen a pro athlete play their game live, or seen a martial artist execute a technique, or watched a Cirque du Soleil performer complete a combination of acrobatic moves? I am sure you have. It is mesmerizing, inspirational, and magnetic! That is how we feel when we are in the presence of those who have Swagger. Their extreme skills are what command our attention, respect and admiration.

As I watched this clown in amazement, I could not help but reminisce about a brief yet powerful discussion with Randy during my most formative years of learning to live with Swagger.

"Joe," he said, "The world meets no one halfway. What I mean is that when it comes to building and living a sales career and life of abundance, it is inherent upon you and you alone to pay the dues to become the best. I have taught you what to say and how to say the words that are embodied in a masterful sales presentation, but it is up to you to internalize them. You must script out exactly how best to present each new blockbuster book to such an extent that nothing is left to chance. The presentation stage of the sales call is show time and it is your time to dance!"

Strategic Sales Presentations: The Key to the Power of Persuasion

Once you have opened the lines of communication with rapport, broke preoccupation with your Transitional Success Story, and completed a thorough qualify, you are ready to tell your story. It is "show time" and you are the lead performer.

The key to developing a successful sales presentation is directly related to the amount of time you spend in preparation. Always remember:

"Prior Planning Prevents Poor Performance."

The five P's consistently apply to all sales professionals who have the desire to become top producers and master the skills essential to those with sales Swagger.

Swag-Step 1: The Goal of the Strategic Sales Presentation

The goal of the presentation stage to the sales process is to bridge the chasm that you have created in the qualify, making your solution/recommendation the most logical option for filling that gap.

Swag-Step 2: The Best Practices of a Strategic Sales Presentation

Developing a strategic sales presentation for your product or service requires strict attention to the following areas:

I.   Addressing the Self-Image of the Prospect
II. Selling Benefits versus Features
III. Multi-Sensory Selling
IV. Strategically Communicating Your Sales Message

Clearly understanding and addressing each of these areas will allow you to build a sales presentation of unequaled persuasive power.

I. Addressing the Self-Image of the Prospect

A strategic sales presentation constructed to Swagger appeals to the self-image of the prospect. The reason this is important is that almost every decision a person makes is fueled by emotion, and this emotion is in direct response to their self-image.

From a sales perspective, a person's self-image is made up of two parts:

1. The way they see themselves
2. The way they want to be seen by others

As you develop your sales presentation, it is important to consider how you are addressing each of these modes of a prospect's self-image. It is always the key to delivering an emotionally charged presentation.

The secret to self-image selling is to understand that people use different modes, or in some cases a combination of these modes, when buying products or services. However, for each purchasing decision, a prospect will tend to focus more on one mode than another.

By asking questions during the qualifying stage of the sales interview, you will get a feel for the dominant self-image the prospect is using to make this particular buying decision. Once identified, it is important to emphasize this self-image mode during the development and implementation of your sales presentation.

Let us look at an example to clarify this concept.

A young salesperson was selling to a prospect who had recently started a new business venture. The salesperson believed the prospect was on a limited budget and unable to purchase the brand new equipment. However, once the salesperson qualified the prospect, she realized that although he was on a limited budget, he was extremely concerned about the way both his new and existing clients viewed his new company. By focusing in on the prospect's self-image, she was able to identify his emotional driver and upgrade him to top-of-the-line equipment. Why did this work so handily? Because it directly addressed his emotional driver: his self-image, and how his clients would see him, an insight that—if overlooked—may not have resulted in a sale at all. Simply put, it was a better fit to what he really wanted, not pegged only to what he needed. Both are critical to making sales. In addition, her astute actions doubled the dollar size of the order and the dollar amount of her commission.

Isn't it true that some people you know care a great deal about how other people view them, while others care very little, if at all? Masters of persuasion are masters of presenting in the self-image mode that is most important to each prospect.

Events, situations and circumstances influence which self-image mode will dominate the decision-making process. The key to identifying the dominant mode is to listen carefully to the answer your prospect gives to the question, "Why is this important? " during the qualifying process. In the majority of cases, this response will clearly illustrate which mode of self-image is dominant—because they will provide clear signs once you train your eyes and ears to notice that they will tell you either what it will mean to "them" or what it will mean to "others."

Swag-Hint

As you can see, it is critical to first identify the dominant self-image mode of your prospect and then direct your entire presentation in a manner that appeals to that mode.

II. Selling Benefits versus Features

A strategic sales presentation is built around the features and benefits of your product/service that directly appeal to the self-image (either the way they see themselves or the way they want others to see them) of your prospect. First, let us clarify what we mean by features and benefits.

Features - All products and services have what are known as salient features. They are the factual characteristics of the product/service that you are offering to the purchaser (like selling cable services: Internet access, phone service, digital cable, and so on).

It is important to identify all of the salient features of the product/ service you are selling. The Action Step in the next few pages will help you prepare this list. It is also important to identify any feature that stands out over those of your competitors. These special features will provide you with what is known as a "Differential Advantage." For example, when the Chrysler Corporation first introduced driver airbags, they had a differential advantage over their competitors who did not offer this feature yet. It was a huge feature, especially to those consumers who valued protecting the life of "self" and/or saw themselves as the protector of others (at least, that's how a Swagger Seller would have seen and described it).

Benefits - Strategic sales presentations are communicated in terms of benefits. Benefits are the value and utility that a prospect will personally derive from purchasing your product/service. A common mistake that salespeople make is to deliver a sales presentation that communicates only the features while ignoring the benefits of the product.

By going the extra mile and explaining how the prospect's self-image will personally benefit from purchasing your product/service, you take a sterile and often boring presentation and pump it full of emotion. One of the greatest reasons why most salespeople sell features vs. benefits is because they do not understand that the focus of benefit-selling is to address the emotional drivers (self-image) of the decision maker.

Your presentation answers the subconscious question that all prospects have, "What's in it for me?" Remember, people make buying decisions based on emotions rather than logical facts, and these emotions are directly linked to the basic motivations of the self-image. Therefore, a picture-perfect sales presentation is made vibrantly colorful and full of emotion by focusing on how your product/service will benefit the prospect's self-image.

Let us look at two different salespeople's presentations in order to illustrate the differences between selling features and selling benefits.

Salesperson #1: Selling Office Equipment Solutions

"Jim, our new product line offers all the latest technological advances - color print capability, duplexing, finishing, scanning and all with an exceptional speed. This unit is just right for you and your business." Notice that the salesperson is delivering a sales presentation focused exclusively on features.

Salesperson #2: Selling Office Equipment Solutions

"Jim, there are many reasons our product is appropriate for you, particularly because of the drive you shared with me to be the best! To begin, this unit offers you the ability to duplex your documents. Being able to print on both sides of the page will save you significantly on your paper cost, particularly when you are doing those multi-page proposals that you told me about earlier. In addition, the finishing capabilities of this product will allow you to dramatically improve the professional look and feel of your proposals. What this will do is give you that slight edge over the lower quality proposals that your competitors are using, and other marketing materials. Last but not least, the speed of this unit will allow you the freedom and flexibility to print those proposals out when it is most convenient for you, even at the last minute. One of the biggest challenges with those slow XYZ brand ink jet printers is that they just take too long to output those critical documents. Nobody wants to be a time slave to their printer." Notice that this salesperson has delivered a sales presentation focused on personal benefits.

Swag-Hint

Powerful presentations link a product's benefits with the prospect's emotional wants.

When it comes time to make a purchase, from whom do you feel Jim will be more inclined to buy the equipment from?

> ### *Swag-Hint*
>
> *Once you have developed a sales presentation focused on benefits, it is important to discuss only those benefits that will directly appeal to the needs and self-image of the prospect to whom you are selling. It is not uncommon for a salesperson to lose the interest of a prospect by discussing features and benefits that are not important to the prospect.*

Action Step

List all the salient features of your product/service. Place a star next to any features you identify that provide you with a potential differential advantage over your main competition.

1.

2.

3.

4.

5.

6.

7.

Action Step

What benefits will the prospect potentially derive from each feature of your product or service?

Feature 1:
Benefit

Feature 2:
Benefit

Feature 3:
Benefit

Feature 4:
Benefit

Feature 5:
Benefit

Feature 6:
Benefit

Feature 7:
Benefit

Swag-Hint

As you think and identify the key benefits to each feature above, remember that each benefit must be articulated to the dominant mode of self-image to which the prospect is emotionally most connected: "self" or "how others see them."

III. Multi-Sensory Selling

The more human senses you involve in your sales presentation, the greater your odds are of making a sale. Everything your prospect experiences and learns is through their senses. As a salesperson, your goal is to trigger a positive response from as many senses as possible. Therefore, strategic sales presentations involve as many of the prospect's senses as possible every time the opportunity presents itself.

By building a presentation based on positive sensory inputs, you greatly enhance the likelihood of receiving a positive response at the conclusion of your presentation.

For example, one extremely successful mobile telephone salesperson absolutely insisted that every potential prospect that comes into the store experiences a hands-on demo of the recommended unit. Rather than just talking to the prospect about the features and benefits of the phone, he ensures that each prospect actually sees, hears and touches them on their own.

Swag-Hint

By involving the senses, you are able to place each prospect strategically in a position of ownership. Helping each prospect see and feel themselves in a position of ownership of the product/service you are marketing will demonstrably improve the power and effectiveness of your sales message.

Action Step

Examine your current sales presentation for opportunities to increase the sensory involvement of your prospect. What specific things could you do to increase your prospect's sensory involvement?

1.

2.

3.

4.

5

6.

7.

8.

9.

10.

IV. Strategically Communicating Your Sales Message

Think of the most successful people you know with careers in acting, politics, law, athletic coaching, teaching, managing or virtually any other professional career. Invariably, they are men and women who are masters of communication. If you are going to climb to the top of the sales profession, you will need to constantly improve your ability to communicate. On the following pages are a few ideas/tips that will enable you to develop and communicate a powerful and persuasive sales message.

A. Painting Mental Pictures for Your Prospect

As human beings, we all tend to think in pictures. As a professional salesperson who knows this, whenever possible, you should use words and phrases that conjure up mental images in the prospect's mind—the kind of colorful communication that screams "Swagger." For example, an unprepared financial salesperson would say to a client, "Let's put this new financial plan in place and get your money working for you." On the other hand, a well-prepared financial salesperson armed with the knowledge we have discussed might say, "Jim, you work hard for your money, it's about time we put a pair of overalls on your money and really get it working for you." Notice how the first example does not really conjure up a mental image while the second example does. The most effective sales presentations incorporate the concept of word pictures.

Action Step

Review your written presentation and look for opportunities to inject words and phrases that will conjure up positive images and emotions in the mind of your prospect. What are some phrases you could use to evoke positive emotional responses?

1.

2.

3.

4.

5

6.

7.

8.

9.

10.

B. Nothing Sells Like a Story

Almost from birth, we are conditioned to listen to stories. As such, nothing grabs the attention and conjures up more positive emotions than the use of a well-told story. Therefore, whenever it is appropriate, you should use this highly effective means of communication to illustrate the key benefit of your product or service.

For example, a salesperson selling medical devices could share a story about how they had helped a similar medical practice. To illustrate this point, the salesperson could tell a story similar to this one: "Last year, I was working in a territory on the other side of the country, and I was referred to a practice just like yours. When I went in, they already recognized that the blood pressure measuring device they were using was not durable and after moderate use was not taking accurate readings. Our Pressure Pro has been battle-tested in the field for a decade and comes with an industry benchmark warranty of three years. This not only helped them save on huge repair and replacement dollars, it gave each doctor in the practice peace of mind that it was accurate when using it with their patients."

C. Mirroring Your Prospect's Style

As we discussed in Chapter 9: The Secret to Establishing Rapport, it is important to mirror your communication style after the person with whom you are speaking. The greatest presentation in the world will yield poor results if it is not packaged and delivered in a way that your prospect can and will accept.

D. Strategic Word Selection

Taking the time to write out your entire sales presentation allows you to carefully choose the words you will use when telling your story. One sales manager, who asked her sales force to write out their presentations, was amazed at how the written presentations differed from the verbal ones she had listened to in the field. The majority of the written presentations were much more thorough and compelling. When she asked each salesperson about the differences in the written and verbal presentations, they commented on how putting their presentation on paper made them really consider what they were saying and how they were saying it.

When writing your actual sales presentation, make a special effort to choose words that do not consciously or subconsciously put your prospect on the defensive. A few commonly used defensive statements are:

"To be honest with you." (This statement implies that the salesperson is not always honest.) An alternative way to say this is: "To be candid with you..."

"The cost is..." (People do not like to incur costs. However, they do like to make investments.) An alternative way to say this is: "The investment is..."

"I need your signature..." (Asking for a signature can cause a prospect to become defensive because they feel they are being pressured into a commitment. However, people do like to feel as though they are in control and important.) An alternative way to ask would be: "I need your approval on this line..."

"The price of the service is $200 down and monthly lease payments of $297.00..." An alternative way to say this is: "The best part about this service is that it is yours with just $200 down and monthly installments of just $297."

Swag-Hint

As you read some of the Power Phrase suggestions above, you might feel they are a little basic or simple. However, I remind you that all those who learn to Swagger focus on mastering the basics!

Action Step

Carefully review your written presentation. Remove any words or phrases that are likely to place your prospect in a defensive position.

What are the phrases or words that you use in your presentation that place the prospect on the defensive?

How can you swap out these defense-driven words/phrases and replace them with empowering words/phrases?

1.	1.
2.	2.
3.	3.
4.	4.
5	5.
6.	6.
7.	7.
8.	8.
9.	9.
10.	10.

E. The Impact of Enthusiasm on Your Sales Presentation

Have you ever watched somebody talk about something they are truly passionate about? Their enthusiasm is captivating. In fact, people cannot help but to be drawn in by what they are saying. Top producing salespeople who move with Swagger possess a passion about what they do and how they are able to help their prospects. This enthusiasm shows through in every word that they speak. As a result, people cannot help but to be drawn to follow the recommendations that these professional salespeople recommend.

There is no refuting that passion and enthusiasm sell. So, how do you go about developing a passion for what you do and an enthusiasm for your product or service? Creating passion and enthusiasm begins by constantly reminding yourself of the benefits of your product or service. Condition yourself to look through your client's eyes. Think of the challenges and frustrations that they face each day, then remind yourself of how your product or service improves the lives of your clients.

One successful sales manager had each sales rep read testimonial letters every morning. As the sales reps read the letters, they were reminded of the true impact that they had on the people who purchased from their company. Over a period of time, the sales reps could not help but become passionate and enthusiastic ambassadors for the company's product. Ultimately, this strategy yielded a sales force that was virtually unstoppable within their industry.

F. Understanding the Power of Non-Verbal Communication

Research has shown that almost 80% of all communication is done non-verbally. With this fact in mind, it is easy to see how a considerable amount of your preparation should be spent on how you will deliver the presentation you have developed. What will you wear? Where will you sit? How will you use your voice, eyes and body language? When you consider the impact of non-verbal communication, it is amazing how little time is spent on enhancing this skill. The Action Step below will provide you with some exercises to improve your non-verbal skills.

Action Step

Now that you have developed a well-thought-out presentation, you are ready to begin working on the most important aspect of your sales message: the non-verbal message. Here are a few techniques that will improve your non-verbal skills:

1. Practice your presentation in the mirror for a week. Pay particular attention to your body movements and gestures. They should be complementing your words.
2. Make an audio recording of your presentation. Listen to the inflections in your voice. Are they consistent with your sales message?
3. Now that we all have the ability to make a video using our phones, tablets or laptops, an excellent way to improve your body language is to make a video of your presentation. Do this periodically and compare new videos with old ones to see how much you've improved and where you can continue to make positive changes.

A Summary of Swagger Fundamentals for Presenting

- The goal of the presentation is to bridge the chasm you created in the qualify; making your solution the most logical option for filling that gap.
- Always appeal to the self-image of the prospect (the way the prospect sees themself, or the way they want to be seen by others). People act/buy on emotions.
- Sell benefits versus features.
- Trigger a positive response from as many senses as possible.
- Use persuasive communication techniques:
    - Paint mental pictures for your prospect with your words
    - Infuse energy and clarity with a story
    - Mirror your prospect's communication style
    - Strategically select the words you use to create mental momentum
    - Enthusiasm always sells
    - Understand and utilize the power of non-verbal communication

Swag-Step 4: The Swagger-Set Diagnostic Tool

The Power of Reflection

Only by truly establishing where you are now, can you crystallize your path forward to total sales mastery.

Identify your Trigger Traits

When it comes to your efforts so far to refine and master the fundamental and critical skill of presenting, which words best describe your behavior? (circle all that apply)

Trigger Traits of Success	Trigger Traits of Failure
↑	↑
Swagger-Set (Optimal Core Beliefs)	No-Swagger (Limiting Beliefs)
Creative	Indifferent
Imaginative	Unimaginative
Positive	Negative
Persistent	Easily Discouraged
Resilient	Defeatist
Adaptive	Inability to Adapt/Change and Grow
Determined	Wavering
Courageous	Fearful
Confident	Lack of Confidence
Takes Initiative	Trapped by Inertia
Self-Reliant	Dependent
Self-Motivated	Lack of Motivation
Accept Personal Responsibility	Lack of Personal Responsibility
Abundant Mentality	Scarcity Mentality

Identify your Core Beliefs

Circle which beliefs you know are helping you take the action needed to master this fundamental and critical skill: presenting.

Remember: Trigger Traits—for success or failure—are the outward reflection of your inner core beliefs.

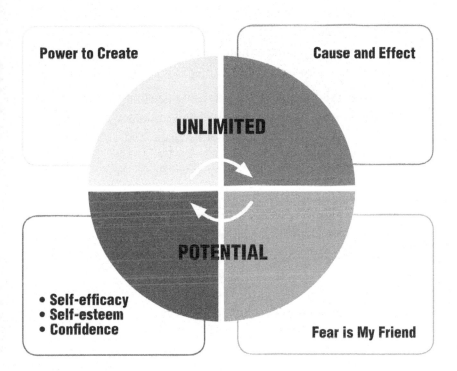

- **Power to Create:** If I cannot see myself, first, as the best, I cannot become the best. All success is created/ envisioned in my mind's eye first.

- **Unlimited Potential:** If I do not believe I can grow, change, adjust and "become," I will not persevere and work tirelessly to master the fundamental skills of my trade. We must believe we can before we will do the things we need to do.

- **Cause & Effect:** If I do not believe that all success is a function of cause and effect, I will focus on the wrong tasks and never consistently execute the right strategies (best practices) essential to my success. As such, I will fail to accept personal responsibility for my results (strong or weak).

- **Self-Efficacy/Self-Esteem:** I must see all feedback in life as not good or bad, but simply information to tap my potential. Otherwise, I will never persevere, remain positive and committed to skill mastery and achievement of my goals.

- **Fear is My Friend:** If I fail to recognize that fear is not my enemy but my friend, I will fail to dream, try new things, and execute on the ideas, plans and strategies needed to succeed.

Action Step: Reflect, Adjust, Succeed

Based upon your identified beliefs and traits, take a moment now to complete your reflection and determine your path forward with the exercise below.

When it comes to the fundamentals/Best Practices needed to master presenting:

I. What Have I Done Right?

II. What Have I Done Wrong?

III. What Will I Do Differently?

Chapter 12:

CLOSING YOUR WAY TO THE TOP—THE PLACE WHERE ALL THOSE WITH SWAGGER SIT

Closing: The Natural Ending to an Orderly Progression

Spring was in the air, and as Randy liked to put it, "The big thaw has begun. Some time in June or July, the snow will be all gone, Joe, and you will be able to see the ground again, ha ha!" as we tossed his bags into the company car and shuffled back off to Buffalo.

I do have to admit that in most years, the snow on the ground actually does not disappear until mid-April. But as always and still to this day, Randy just can't help but take a jab...I love hating these Swagger people!

We jumped up on the expressway and settled into our sixty-minute drive of what salespeople and sales managers affectionately refer to as "windshield time." As you and I know, a great deal of professional and personal growth happens during this time, because if you are alone, you can have time to reflect —and if you are with your mentor, you can be thrown right back into boot camp and be pushed mentally and conditioned physically with countless role plays and rehearsals of sales interviews. At least, that is how I viewed it.

"So how goes it this morning, JoJo?" he asked.

Not really putting much weight on what I said, he already was reading me...my non-verbal communication, my body language, breathing, voice inflections, every facet of communication, which he taught me to do as well.

"I'm great, Randy, how are you?" I fired back—that's what you do in boot camp, and I was about to be mentally mixed to be weapons-grade capable in my thinking and skill capacity…again.

"You do not seem great this morning. You look a little uncomfortable, and I don't think it is because Macmillan has us two six-footers stuffed into this death sled they call a car," the Pontiac J2000 at the time.

He was right, the motorized go-cart I had as a young teenager was bigger than this thing. I shifted to my other side to let the feeling back into my legs.

"What's on your mind, my man?" he asked as he dug in, while I looked for higher mental ground…which I could rarely if ever find when we trained.

I came clean. "I am a little anxious (to say the least) about our visit to SUNY Buffalo today. We have a huge adoption"— if you remember, this is what they call a sale in the college textbook industry—"pending on our intro to sociology book by Conklin, and I am as nervous as a young buck on prom night." I smiled at my own joke as I glanced over, waiting for his response.

"Hah!" He laughed out loud as he spooled up for his response. "Why are you so nervous? Have you built great rapport this semester with the professor?"

"Heck, yeah!" I fired back. "She is a great lady, smart as a whip and she herself has written several books, one in particular about Love Canal, about the huge contamination by a big chemical manufacturer of an entire neighborhood. I was genuinely interested in the subject, so I bought her book and read it."

"Really," Randy said with a smile of approval. "And did you discuss the book with her?"

"Oh yeah," I replied, "she was taken aback that I showed such an interest, and it turned out we had a bunch of common moral beliefs about corporate responsibility regarding safety." I shifted my weight again to get the blood flowing down to my legs.

"So, seems like you have built terrific and genuine rapport with her," he said.

"I sure have. She is great, and I think she thinks well of me, too."

He started asking his next questions slowly, the way he always did when taking an opportunity to train me. "Were you able to qualify her with regard to the book she is currently using as a teaching tool with the students, and create a genuine chasm of how the Conklin book could help her teach and the students learn more effectively next semester?"

I nodded. "For sure. She teaches the course from a conflict resolution (buzz words for this particular subject) perspective and it was her biggest interest and challenge," I said with a smile and a little release of pent-up steam.

"How did your presentation of the actual book go?" The book presentation is known as the walk-through in textbook sales. "Were you able to bridge the chasm you created with your walk-through of the book?"

"I sure did. She really liked the way Conklin covered the topic and felt it would really be an asset to both her teaching and the students' learning."

"Excellent!" he said. "So what are you nervous about?"

I pondered for a moment, then said, "Today I have to ask her for an actual commitment to adopt the book next semester."

"So visualize with me," Randy said. "What is she going to do?"

"I believe she is going to adopt Conklin and put me over my sales quota for the year."

Randy asked, "Why? Why is she going to do that?"

"Because I earned the right to get her business. Conklin is a great fit for her and the students."

"Then I agree," Randy said, nodding, "that is what she will do. Statistically speaking," he waxed on, "if you go through each stage [or what he often called the gate] of the sales process— Rapport, Transitional Success Story, Qualify, and Presentation at the highest level of execution—the Closing stage is nothing to fear and nothing to shy away from. It is the natural ending to an orderly progression."

He continued, "The sale is always made in your mind first, Joe, as the professional salesperson. You decide, as the expert, if the product/service, or in this case the Conklin book, is a good fit by conducting a powerful sales interview. And if it is, the master of closing need not fret about asking for the order. In fact, as a master, you are not asking at all. What you are doing is simply articulating to the prospect the decision you have already made in your mind's eye—like we just did by visualizing now—and simply soliciting their agreement to your recommendation."

As I placed the car in park and opened the door to begin our day, I felt the pressure slip away as we Swaggered our way together toward the student center for our caffeine fix, and finalize our plan of attack for the day.

The first step towards becoming a master closer is to realize that, as a professional salesperson, you not only have the right to close, you have an obligation. Once you have successfully completed each of the previous stages in the sales process, closing is the natural ending to an orderly progression.

Swag Step 1: The Goal of the Closing Stage

In the world of professional sales, one of the greatest misconceptions, held by both salespeople and managers alike, is the belief that closing is the art of getting a prospect to make a decision to buy. In reality, nothing could be further from the truth. Remember, in professional sales we sell only to people that we can truly help. It is at the conclusion of a thorough qualify that you, the salesperson, decide whether or not your product or service can meet the needs and wants of the prospect. As a result, the decision to buy is actually made in your mind first. In other words, the key to closing is for you to make the decision for the prospect to buy and then focus the balance of the presentation on persuading the prospect to agree with your decision.

Swag-Hint

The goal of closing is selling yourself, first, that your recommendation is right for them; then simply having the prospect agree with your decision.

Although this theory may seem in drastic contrast to what you have learned in the past, be assured it is the key to mastering the power of persuasion. If you understand and internalize this concept, you will be well on the way to Closing Your Way to the Top—the place where those with Swagger always sit.

Swag-Step 2: The Best Practices/Strategies to Closing

The Trial Close

All successful closers begin closing early in the sales presentation with a subtle strategy called the trial close. When used strategically, trial closes are very powerful tools that greatly enhance the positive outcome of your sales presentation.

Trial closes serve two primary purposes. First, they enable you to take periodic temperature checks to make sure your prospect is comprehending the sales message and staying emotionally involved. Second, trial closes build a positive momentum of "yes" answers or approval from the prospect. Remembering what we discussed earlier, the key to closing is getting the prospect to agree with the buying decision you have made for them. By getting the prospect accustomed to agreeing early in your presentation, trial closing becomes a critical prelude to the close. The most effective place to begin your trial close strategy is at the end of the qualify. Then continue using trial closes throughout the balance of your sales presentation. Let us look at two trial close strategies that will immediately enhance your closing prowess.

I. The Take-Away Trial Close

Frequently using a "take-away" or reverse psychology approach can move a prospect toward your way of thinking. This strategy is extremely effective when used at the end of the qualifying stage to start building positive momentum and to solicit a commitment to take action at the conclusion of the presentation you are about to deliver. For example, an insurance agent may want to consider using a take-away trial close such as, "Jim, many people that I talk with are just not serious about strengthening the financial position of their company, are you really sincere about wanting to protect your assets, and about saving money? Excellent! I have a plan that will help you. Let 's take a look at it."

Another example that highlights this strategy is: "Mary and Bob, many new businesses want to purchase the best advertising possible, but when it comes right down to it they just aren't ready to make a commitment. If I can show you an advertising solution that fits within your budget and meets the criteria you have shared with me, are you committed to making a change? Outstanding, then let's get started! I have a solution that is perfect for your organization."

II. The Common Sense Trial Close

The common sense trial close is used primarily to solicit a "yes" answer. Using this strategy in your presentation accomplishes three things: it builds positive momentum, keeps the prospect mentally engaged and provides you with valuable feedback. For example, "Jim, you can see how new bundled Internet services will increase your speed of transmission and reduce your costs starting next month, isn't that right? The only thing we need to get started is…"

Action Step

Review your presentation and incorporate trial closes at the end of your qualify and throughout the body of your presentation using the "Take-Away" and the "Common Sense" strategies. What are some trial closes that would work well with your product/service presentation?

1.

2.

3.

Developing a Closing Mix

In the field of professional sales, fortunes are lost because salespeople fail to recognize the need for developing and utilizing a closing mix— meaning, the need to use more than one closing technique.

Most salespeople have one, or in rare cases, two closes they use to consummate a sale. However, it has been statistically proven that most sales do not take place until the fourth or fifth closing attempt. Therefore, to have a closing arsenal with only one or two closes is not a good strategy at all. If you intend to be a master salesperson, you must be prepared to close for the order at least five times during your closing presentation.

A number of years ago, *Selling* magazine did a study on a prospect's impression of a salesperson's closing strategy. Interestingly, prospects viewed salespeople who closed for the order two times as being pushy and aggressive. Conversely, salespeople who closed five or more times were viewed as having a deep belief in the value of their product or service. The same study found that the average salesperson uses just two closing attempts. As a result, fortunes are left on the closing table.

Many times salespeople are reluctant to close for the order more than two times for fear of being viewed as too aggressive. According to *Selling*, the exact opposite is true; and according to those with Swagger, we don't question the formula that works. We master it!

Swag-Hint

Top salespeople carry with them an unstoppable closing mix comprised of at least five closing tracks.

Building Your Closing Arsenal

Those who sell with Swagger never rely on a closing strategy that is comprised of a single close (no more than Michael Jordan or Kobe Bryant has one approach to the basket). Rather, the best salespeople utilize a strategy made up of a vast arsenal of closes. Let us examine several different closing methods that you can use to develop a winning closing strategy.

I. The Assumptive Close Misconception

The very nature of true professional/consultative selling dictates that all closes should be assumptive. If you have completed a thorough qualify and have made the decision to do a sales presentation, then you have already assumed the prospect will want to buy from you. Remember, *the art of closing is not to get the prospect to make a buying decision. As a sales professional, you make the decision to buy and then deliver the balance of the presentation assuming the prospect will agree.* Therefore, when a sales interview is conducted with true professional (consultative) intentions, it is only natural and logical to conclude that all closes are assumptive.

II. The Alternate Choice Close

The alternate choice close consists of you asking the prospect to choose between two decisions that will ultimately result in the prospect agreeing to buy your service/product. For example:

"Which is better for you, Mr. Jones, the leasing option or the purchase plan?"

III. The Paperwork Close

This close simply consists of the salesperson physically beginning to fill out the necessary paperwork at the conclusion of a masterful presentation. For example:

"Steve, I will submit the mortgage application before we end our visit today, and we should have a preliminary commitment within 24 hours. Before I hit submit, I need a little information to complete the application. What is the business address?"

IV. The Minor Point Close

The minor point close is an extremely effective close in almost all situations. This type is again, assumptive by nature, and consists of the salesperson asking the prospect a minor question. When the prospect answers the question they concede to making the purchase. For example: "Jim, would you prefer to do the training on your new medical equipment next Wednesday or Thursday?"

V. The Benefit versus Loss Close

In this close the salesperson tactfully points out how the prospect will gain a benefit and/or avoid a loss through the purchase of the product or service. Remember, at the very foundation of human motivation all purchasing decisions are ultimately made to gain a benefit or to avoid a loss. The prospect is always asking himself, "What's in it for me?" This closing strategy enables you to address these basics of human motivation directly.

"Mark, I know that the budget is tight right now and that you have to make a move to upgrade your equipment. Occasionally, we will take equipment in on trade, fully recondition it and offer it for sale. Just yesterday, we took in a two-year machine that I think will match perfectly what you are looking for. This is a great machine, but I can't guarantee it will last for long in our warehouse. Let's fill out the paperwork today, and that way I can assure you don't miss out on this great opportunity. What is the best number for me to reach you at for final confirmation?"

VI. The Storybook Close

This technique consists of you telling the prospect a story with a Hollywood ending. The story might be about a past client who is similar to the prospect and has reaped tremendous benefits because they purchased your product or service. Remember, people think in pictures and make decisions based on emotion. An effective storybook close accomplishes both, thus this is one of the most powerful closing techniques you can develop and use.

One of my close friends and a client for many years is an accomplished writer of many books. She used this exact technique, telling a prospect about the success of one of her books in a similar situation: "Mark, I want to bring this book to your attention because just last month, a public radio station in a major market used it as a premium, and it brought in 500 new members. I want to be sure you have the same opportunity to expand your audience by using this book as a gift." The prospect placed an order with her on the spot. That's the strength of the Hollywood ending!

Creating a Closing Sequence

The closing methods described above are proven techniques that you can apply to enhance your closing abilities immediately and get your Swagger on. However, the real power of these closes is found when you develop a closing sequence. As you recall, most sales are not made until the salesperson has made the fourth or fifth closing attempt. Taking the time to organize these closes into a strategic sequence will ensure you the outstanding results you desire.

Swag-Hint

Although your closing sequence should take into account your individual style and product/service, here are a few ideas you will want to give serious thought to as you create your closing sequence:

1. Remember, you, not the prospect, make the buying decision during the qualifying stage of your sales interview. Therefore, all closes employed at the conclusion of your sales presentation are assumptive by design.

2. At the conclusion of your sales presentation, it is often effective to begin your closing sequence by employing a closing strategy that offers the prospect a choice. Either an Alternative Choice strategy such as the type of payment, "Did the lease or purchase option work better for you?" or a Minor Point choice such as, "Would you prefer the training to be early or late next week?"

3. *If applicable, the Paperwork close should be used in unison with all of the closing strategies you employ. In the majority of sales, paperwork needs to be completed to facilitate the sale. Many times, salespeople erroneously wait for the prospect to commit to a purchase before beginning to gather the information needed. Instead, top closers keep all applicable forms in clear view, either in hand or on their laptop/tablet screen. When they reach the closing stage of the sales interview, they use these forms to complement their closing efforts. For example in the Alternative Choice example used above, "No problem, Jim, I will get the leasing paperwork submitted today. What is your Employer Identification Number?"*

4. *The Storybook close and the Benefit versus Loss closing strategies are extremely effective when used in the latter part of your closing sequence. This is because these closes enable you to create strong emotion and provide your prospect with the reassurance that is typically needed when a quality prospect continues to hesitate.*

Find any top producing sales professional who moves with Swagger, and you will discover a salesperson who has developed the ability to close. If you believe in your product/service and have thoroughly completed each stage of the sales process, you have earned the right to close. A closing strategy consisting of a five part closing sequence will ensure you are on track to closing your way to the top ranks of your profession—the place where all those that "Swagger Sell" sit!

Action Step

In the space provided below, develop your closing sequence using the strategies you learned in this lesson.

1.

2.

3.

4.

5.

A Summary of Swagger Fundamentals for Closing

- The decision to buy is always made in you, the salesperson's, mind first.
- Use trial closes to take periodic temperature checks of your prospect, and build positive momentum by soliciting "yes"/"acknowledgment."
- Create a closing mix comprised of 5 strategic closes.
- Most sales are not consummated until the fourth or fifth close.

Swag-Step 4: The Swagger-Set Diagnostic Tool

The Power of Reflection

Only by truly establishing where you are now, can you crystallize your path forward to total sales mastery.

Identify your Trigger Traits

When it comes to your efforts so far to refine and master the fundamental and critical skill of closing, which words best describe your behavior? (circle all that apply)

Trigger Traits of Success ⬆ Swagger-Set (Optimal Core Beliefs)	Trigger Traits of Failure ⬆ No-Swagger (Limiting Beliefs)
Creative	Indifferent
Imaginative	Unimaginative
Positive	Negative
Persistent	Easily Discouraged
Resilient	Defeatist
Adaptive	Inability to Adapt/Change and Grow
Determined	Wavering
Courageous	Fearful
Confident	Lack of Confidence
Takes Initiative	Trapped by Inertia
Self-Reliant	Dependent
Self-Motivated	Lack of Motivation
Accept Personal Responsibility	Lack of Personal Responsibility
Abundant Mentality	Scarcity Mentality

Identify your Core Beliefs

Circle which beliefs you know are helping you take the action needed to master this fundamental and critical skill: closing.

Remember: *Trigger Traits—for success or failure—are the outward reflection of your inner core beliefs.*

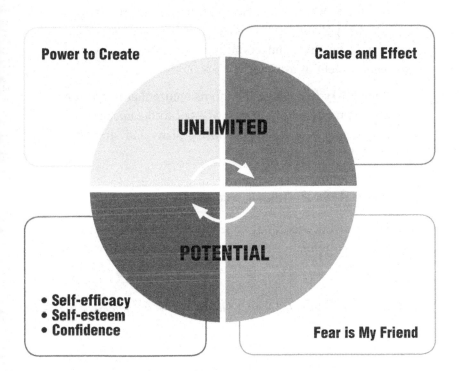

- **Power to Create:** If I cannot see myself, first, as the best, I cannot become the best. All success is created/ envisioned in my mind's eye first.

- **Unlimited Potential:** If I do not believe I can grow, change, adjust and "become," I will not persevere and work tirelessly to master the fundamental skills of my trade. We must believe we can before we will do the things we need to do.

- **Cause & Effect:** If I do not believe that all success is a function of cause and effect, I will focus on the wrong tasks and never consistently execute the right strategies (best practices) essential to my success. As such, I will fail to accept personal responsibility for my results (strong or weak).

- **Self-Efficacy/Self-Esteem:** I must see all feedback in life as not good or bad, but simply information to tap my potential. Otherwise, I will never persevere, remain positive and committed to skill mastery and achievement of my goals.

- **Fear is My Friend:** If I fail to recognize that fear is not my enemy but my friend, I will fail to dream, try new things, and execute on the ideas, plans and strategies needed to succeed.

Action Step: Reflect, Adjust, Succeed

Based upon your identified beliefs and traits, take a moment now to complete your reflection and determine your path forward with the exercise below.

When it comes to the fundamentals/Best Practices needed to master closing:

I. What Have I Done Right?

II. What Have I Done Wrong?

III. What Will I Do Differently?

Chapter 13:

OVERCOMING SALES OBJECTIONS/RESISTANCE

A Curve in the Close

As we knocked on Professor Smith's* office door later that morning, I could still feel the swarm of butterflies swirling around in my stomach.

"Come on in, Joe," she said with a smile. "And I see you brought a friend with you."

"Yes, I sure did, Dr. Smith. This is Randy, my manager at Macmillan."

"Pleased to meet you, Randy."

"And you as well, Dr. Smith," Randy said as he slowly sat down, with the calm of a ninja who has already won the war. "How are you doing today?"

"Great," she replied. "Almost done with the semester and I am looking forward to the summer, so I can take a deep breath and enjoy some life off campus. How are the two of you doing today?"

"Fabulous, Dr. Smith. We have but a few weeks to go ourselves, and then we get to join you and all of the professors with a nice summer break." (By the way, did I mention that in the college publishing industry, salespeople received the same down time as the college professors did? Meaning summer, for the most part, was off, except for the company national sales meeting and a few regional meetings.)

"Oh, you get summer break, too?"

"We sure do," Randy joined in. "And it is a fantastic benefit indeed, but after seven years in the industry, I am still not sure it makes up for all the hours in travel and work Joe and I do the rest of the year." We all laughed out loud together.

*Name has been changed to protect privacy

"I feel your pain," she quickly added, with a big smile.

As our discussion moved on, <u>I transitioned with a story</u> that our marketing department had given us about the tremendous success Conklin was having in the marketplace with both professors and students alike. I revisited the discussion we had about Dr. Smith's wants and needs in a new book for her and her students, carefully recreating the chasm of where she was now and where she wanted to go. I reopened the book and carefully described how the Conklin book was both the salvation and rejuvenation of her course next year for both her and her students, placing strong emphasis on the differential advantages Conklin provided because of the way it covered conflict resolution—and even spoke carefully to her esteem, which was clearly her desire to be and be seen as the best professor she could be.

As I transitioned to the close (my annual sales goal swaying in the air), all hell broke loose.

"Dr. Smith, I am truly excited for you and your new students next year, Conklin is going to be so helpful to you and them. Did you already let the bookstore know you are going to be using a new book"—they were the ones that actually processed the new orders each semester for the professors—"or would you like me to stop by and let them know when I'm there later this afternoon?" (How's that for an example of the alternative choice close?)

"Well, Joe," she began, "I am not sure I will be making the switch this upcoming semester. I may need to postpone it until next springtime." As she spoke, I felt my mind start to panic. Next spring would be a whole year from now.

I kept my cool, I did not even hesitate. I had already been trained and armed with multiple closes and simply flowed to the strong reassurance and minor point close.

"Dr. Smith, you will truly be ecstatic you made the switch for the upcoming fall semester. Keep in mind the Conklin book is significantly more up to date than the current book you are using, and as you have shared with me before, cannot even come close to how well Conklin covers conflict resolution. I will also make sure I get you the extra free copies of the book you need for your teaching assistants. How many will you need?"

Dr. Smith paused for a moment in thought and them slowly replied, "I will need four extra copies."

"Thank God," I said inwardly, only to be jolted again.

She went on, "But I really do not think I have the time to change all of my teaching notes and re-prep my lectures this summer due to other demands on my time. So I think I am going to have to wait."

As she stalled again, I could feel the sweat under my arms start to build and I started fixating on the big gap forming in my sales goal—and not giving a single thought to her needs and wants, a big mental "no-no" to sales success. Bottom line: As a rookie, I started to mentally crumble...and as the butterflies in my stomach started to swirl like a squadron of bees whose hive was just kicked and shattered...I heard the calm voice of Randy chime in with a question.

"Dr. Smith," he said with a warm, friendly smile, "With the exception of the prep-time challenge you just shared, is there any other reason you would not adopt Conklin for this fall?"

She replied, "No, there is no other reason...I really love this new book and I am going to adopt it, but I am taking time this summer to edit my current book for a second edition for my publisher, and I just won't have time to do both. In addition, your rep Joe has done a terrific job with helping me and I really do want to give him this adoption"—I started to breathe again—"but I just can't until next spring."

"Dr. Smith," Randy continued softly, mentally sparring with the professor, "If we were able to eliminate the majority of prep time typically needed to redo your teaching notes and slides, would you throw Joe a bone and adopt Conklin today for the fall?"

Randy always had a way with word pictures and expressions ...and it was a good thing, as I cowered in the chair next to his.

"Well, I definitely would," she replied, "but how can you help me do that?"

"Conklin comes with a complete teacher's guide, and let me tell you, it is robust. It provides all of the teaching lecture notes for each class and even has the slide deck, too. You are going to love it, because you will need to allocate no prep time this summer, and yet, you and your students will experience the best intro to sociology book on the market. Sound like a plan?"

Dr. Smith smiled wide and almost shouted it out. "A great plan indeed, Randy! You have the order, Joe."

As we wrapped up and made our way down the hall to our next call, Randy stopped by an open bench and asked me to sit for a moment.

I was not only accustomed to our development process of reflection, I had come to really appreciate his feedback and insights—and today I had just witnessed a sure sale snatched out of my hands, and then thanks to this truly gifted man, watched it put right back into place.

"Well, that was interesting, wasn't it?" Randy opened the discussion.

"Sure was..." I said with a big sigh of relief.

"Joe, what did you and I as a team do right, what did we do wrong, and most importantly, what did we learn that will help us refine and improve the results we seek—a new sale?"

I realized this process had become almost effortless for both him and me. "We had great rapport," I began. "I reignited her with a new Transitional Success Story with our new marketing report, and I could tell she appreciated seeing it. I re-established the chasm by paraphrasing our qualify, and I bridged it, almost effortlessly, in the presentation stage. All this made the transition to the close unfold exactly how you taught me; it was a natural ending to an orderly progression."

"Exactly," Randy exclaimed. "And I have to say I was truly impressed by the level of perfection you executed each stage. It was top notch...all except the close. Why do I say this, Joe?" he asked in a caring tone.

"Well, you see, Randy, that's what I am unsure about. I did everything right at every stage and I know it. I even didn't flinch when she resisted the first time. I simply reassured her and closed again…but." I paused.

"But what?" Randy asked.

"I paused because I was stunned that she pushed it off twice with the same lame excuse—'I don't have the time to prepare.' And as you saw, I started to freeze."

"Yes, you sure did," Randy said, laughing out loud. "But what do you expect? You live here in this tundra of freezing weather." He laughed even louder before he went on. "But all kidding aside, you froze because you knew if you tried to close again it wouldn't have worked, right?"

"Yes," I said.

"And you even know why, don't you?"

"Yeah, I do. She kept giving me the same objection."

"Which was?"

"I don't have time to make the change this summer. I am re-writing my book."

"Exactly," Randy said again. "Which told you what?"

"It told me that it was a real objection and I needed to use the skill you taught me about how to isolate the objection, overcome it and close again."

"That is correct, my young Jedi. But you did not. Why? Did you not remember the book came with a corresponding teaching guide?"

"No," I replied. "I knew it did. I think I was just frustrated, perhaps afraid and maybe even shocked that she just didn't buy—until you used the technique for overcoming objections we trained on."

And with a smile the size of a half moon, Randy looked at me and simply replied, "You did everything right. She just needed your help to take that final step. It is simply just how sales works. It's part of the process. Always remember, Joe, you are not selling until they are not buying. Overcoming objections and/or resistance in each sales meeting is just another natural part of the sales process. Sort of like the natural transition of the seasons in most parts of the world...except where you live."

He stood up with a huge grin on his face. "Let's go get some lunch."

Swag-Step 1: The Goal of Overcoming Sales Objections

In the world of professional selling, mastering how to overcome sales objections is a critical stage of the sales process and of career success. There is a natural resistance that occurs in a prospect's mind—at times—when you begin your final approach to the closing runway. As such, those with Swagger not only understand the source of objections, they thrive on them—because they know that objections (or what I like to call sales resistance) are simply the navigational lights they need to land the sale.

Swag-Step 2: The Purpose of Overcoming Sales Objections

Few things are more exhilarating or rewarding than mastering the ability to overcome sales objections. In the world of professional sales, the thrill of the chase either begins or ends based on your ability to successfully field and handle objections. If you plan to become a top producer, being able to effectively handle and overcome sales objections is a mandatory skill you simply must master.

The Cause of Sales Objections

In order to solve any problem, you must first understand its cause. Therefore, any discussion of how to overcome sales objections must begin with an understanding of how they are created.

Almost all sales objections can be directly traced back to an infringement of the prospect's self-image (either the way they see themselves, or the way they want others to see them). The theory focuses on the integral role that a prospect's self-image plays in every sales interview. Sales objections are raised when the prospect's self-image has not been properly addressed, or when they perceive that their self-image is at risk of being attacked or challenged.

> *Swag-Hint*
>
> ---
>
> *The majority of sales objections are created by the actions of the salesperson.*

When you look at these reasons, it becomes evident that almost all sales objections can be traced back to the actions and comments of the salesperson during the sales interview. In fact, informal studies have shown that the majority of objections relate directly to the actions and mindset of the salespeople themselves rather than the actual product or service they sell. Let us take a closer look at what causes sales objections to be raised at each stage of the sales process.

I. The Cause of Objections While Building Rapport and Qualifying

The first place in which a salesperson may encounter sales resistance occurs during the initial rapport building or qualifying stage of the sales interview. Remember Dr. X from the Business Department at Brockport College—the one who threw me out of his office? I sure do! Salespeople who encounter objections this early can be assured that the cause of this resistance is:

a. The prospect is not a good candidate for what you are marketing; there are no "needs" that your product/service can satisfy, or the prospect simply cannot afford your product or service.

b. The salesperson has not developed the people skills necessary to command the attention and respect of the prospect. This further lends credence to the saying, "You must first sell yourself before you can sell your product."

More often than not, an objection at this early stage of the sales interview is caused by the latter. A prospect with a strong self-image will not cooperate with salespeople who have not taken the time to polish their sales skills. In this instance, the prospect does not feel that their self-image is enhanced by communicating with the salesperson. Thus, they attempt to terminate the interview with an abrupt objection.

II. The Cause of Objections While Conducting the Sales Presentation

The second place that a salesperson may encounter an objection is during the actual presentation. Objections at this point are typically caused by a failure to thoroughly qualify the prospect. In this scenario, the salesperson has not truly identified the prospect's "wants" and "needs," and therefore is not effectively presenting the product's ability to meet them. These types of objections are typical of a salesperson who has not perfected their questioning techniques and/or listening skills.

It does not matter what the salesperson thinks the prospect's "wants" and "needs" ought to be. Rather, it is **critical** to identify what the prospect perceives as their "wants" and "needs" based on their self-image. If these are not properly identified by a series of thorough qualifying questions, then the sales message cannot be delivered in a way that illustrates how the purchase of your product/service is going to appeal to the prospect.

III. The Cause of Objections While Closing the Sale

The final stage in which you may encounter objections is at the end of the sales interview when you begin the close. Objections at this stage of the sales process are raised for one of two important reasons:

1. The salesperson has not clearly communicated the sales message in a fashion that illustrates how the prospect will gain a benefit or avoid a loss by making a decision to buy. Thus, the prospect is reluctant. If the salesperson has not thoroughly shown how the prospect's self-image will be complemented or preserved, then the sales interview will undoubtedly end short of the sale.

   A salesperson once described how he completed a presentation to an office manager but ultimately lost the sale.

The presentation clearly illustrated how the new cable service would save company employees time and reduce service expenses. The salesperson perceived that the sale was lost because the office manager was lazy and did not want the hassle of making a change. However, after some consideration, it became apparent that the sale was actually lost because the salesperson did not describe how the decision to buy the new service would complement or enhance the office manager's self-image. The key question, "What's in it for me?" was never addressed. Instead, the salesperson closed on how the employees would benefit and how the company would save money. The sale could have been made had the salesperson demonstrated how the purchase would have addressed the motivations of the office manager's self-image.

For example: "John, this new technology in your office will further demonstrate to the company employees that you understand their needs for increased productivity. In addition, this investment will clearly show your boss that you continue to seek out opportunities to save your company time and money."

2. The salesperson has made a thorough presentation and is encountering resistance caused by the natural human defense mechanism triggered when a commitment is solicited from a prospect during the closing stage. *These are the most common types of objections you will encounter once you have mastered the other stages of the sales process.* Typically, these objections occur even when the sales presentation has been effectively executed. The objections you receive at this stage of the sales process are easier to accept when you recognize that it is human nature to resist making decisions. The prospect hesitates because they are still a little unsure how a commitment will impact their self-image. More often than not, reassurance followed by a closing question will complete the sale at this point.

> ### *Swag-Hint*
>
> *Many times the prospect will not have a real objection and the objections are random emotional acts to stall from agreeing with your recommendation. As such, the technique is **not** to isolate but rather simply to reassure and close again.*

An example of this: "Laura, you will always be glad you took this step to protect your family's financial stability and future in the event something happened to you unexpectedly. This policy will provide each of them a roof over their heads, food and education until they are all over 22. Laura, I need your okay on this line."

A second example of this can be found in the sale of the Conklin book. In the case of Dr. Smith and the new textbook, the professor's own need to feel fully prepared for her students prevented her from agreeing to adopt the new book, because she already had a full plate and would not have time over the summer to prepare adequately. Once Randy explained that Macmillan would provide everything she needed and gave her strong reassurance it would make her look great and provide the best teaching tool for her students, she was ready for us to close the sale.

In summary, the foundation of all sales objections is centered around the salesperson's ability to appeal to the emotional desires of the prospect's self-image. Remember, human beings are always motivated to take action for one of two reasons, either to gain a benefit or avoid a loss. However, the gain or loss is not linked to the product or service. It is linked to the product's/service's ability to address the basic motivational drives of the prospect's self-image (how they see themselves, or how they want to be seen by others). More objections are raised, and sales lost, because salespeople fail to recognize how literally every decision that a prospect makes is influenced by the way they see themselves and/or the way they want others around them to see them. In the three examples above:

1. John, the office manager, viewed himself as competent and as such, was motivated to make the purchase because he wanted his associates and the boss to see him this way as well.
2. Laura, the parent and financial provider of her family, views herself as both the provider and the protector of her family's daily lives and future. As such, she was motivated to act by reassurance and appeal to how she sees herself in her parent role.
3. Dr. Smith is committed and sees herself as a great professor, and wants to make sure her students always see her this way, too.

Action Step

Based on what you learned from this chapter, list the objections you typically encounter, and decide what stage of the sales interview they are in (rapport/qualify/presentation/close).

Objection #1:
Stage:

Objection #2:
Stage:

Objection #3:
Stage:

Objection #4:
Stage:

Objection #5:
Stage:

Objection #6:
Stage:

Action Step

If the majority of the sales objections you are getting surface early in your presentation, list some actual steps you will take to:

Make sure you are targeting and approaching the right prospects by:

1.

2.

3.

Improve your skill and professional appearance/demeanor by:

1.

2.

3.

Sharpen the quality and caliber of questions you are using to qualify prospects by:

1.

2

3.

Action Step

If the majority of the sales objections you are receiving are occurring during your presentation stage of your sales interview, list some actual steps you will take to:

Make sure you are truly capturing the wants and needs of your prospect by:

1.

2

3.

Make sure you do not assume the wants and needs of your prospect based on your beliefs, but based on the prospect's beliefs/self-esteem (what they want and care about) by:

1.

2

3.

Swag-Step 3: Best Practices/Strategies to Overcome Sales Objections

The optimum strategy for overcoming sales objections involves three steps. Let's review them together:

Step #1: Once an objection has been raised, allow the prospect to completely voice their opinion. Encourage the prospect to completely open up and express their feelings.

Strategy: Listening carefully to both the words and the emotions of your prospect shows your concern for their feelings. By showing that you legitimately care about them, your prospect feels important, which in turn enhances their self-image.

Step #2: Isolate the objection by asking a qualifying question to ensure you understand the objection.

Strategy: By isolating the objection you illustrate to the prospect your true concern for their needs and worth as an individual.

Step #3: Address the objection directly by answering the question and continue to close.

Swag-Hint

So much of human communication is non-verbal. Your prospect, in almost all cases, is looking for you to acknowledge his concerns. By being direct and confident, you are able to give the prospect peace of mind.

Swag-Hint

It is important to note that many sales are lost because the salesperson failed to ask a closing question after overcoming the objection. By not asking a closing question, rather than reassuring and enhancing the prospect's self-image, you are actually threatening it. The prospect does not feel reassured of their buying decision. Instead they tend to feel that the salesperson has outwitted them and their self-image prompts them to object again. When this takes place, the salesperson and prospect end up in the all too familiar sales game of "ego ping-pong."

Let us illustrate this technique with an example.

Step #1 - Listen and Show Empathy:

Prospect: "I'm afraid I just can't afford to upgrade. We just moved into this new office and the budget is really too tight."

Salesperson: "Jim, I can appreciate your financial concerns with the recent move. In fact, I have several quality clients, just like you, who were under a tight budget when we first sat down."

Step #2 - Isolate the Objection

Salesperson: "Jim, other than the investment portion, is there any other reason you wouldn't want to look into upgrading at this time?"

Prospect: "No."

Step #3 - Answer the Objection and Close

Salesperson: "Well Jim, the investment payments are not engraved in stone. In fact, I am confident I can restructure the finances to make it work within the constraints of your current budget. So I can get you started today I just need to get a little bit more information...."

> ### *Swag-Hint*
>
> *As seen through the story of Dr. Smith at the beginning of the chapter, and as I mentioned above, it is important that the prospect object twice— with the same objection—before you begin to isolate and overcome the objection with the three steps above.*
>
> *Why? Because many times the prospect will not have a real objection and the objections are random emotional acts to stall from agreeing with your recommendation. As such, the technique is **not** to isolate—with the three steps above—but rather simply to reassure and close again.*

Action Step

Using the techniques described in the section on "How To Overcome Objections," develop a response to those objections you are experiencing during the close.

1.

2.

3.

A Summary of Swagger Fundamentals for Overcoming Objections

- Objections are the navigational lights needed to land a sale.
- The majority of sales objections are created by the actions of you, the salesperson.
- Do not address a sales objection until you've heard the same objection twice. Instead, simply reassure and close again. This technique handily removes mere smoke screens.
- When you have encountered a "real" objection take time to:
    - Listen to the prospect and show empathy with their concern.
    - Isolate the objection (example: is there any other reason?).
    - Answer the objection directly and close again immediately.

Swag-Step 4: The Swagger-Set Diagnostic Tool

The Power of Reflection

Only by truly establishing where you are now, can you crystallize your path forward to total sales mastery.

Identify your Trigger Traits

When it comes to your efforts so far to refine and master the fundamental and critical skill of overcoming objections, which words best describe your behavior? (circle all that apply)

Trigger Traits of Success ⬆ Swagger-Set (Optimal Core Beliefs)	Trigger Traits of Failure ⬆ No-Swagger (Limiting Beliefs)
Creative	Indifferent
Imaginative	Unimaginative
Positive	Negative
Persistent	Easily Discouraged
Resilient	Defeatist
Adaptive	Inability to Adapt/Change and Grow
Determined	Wavering
Courageous	Fearful
Confident	Lack of Confidence
Takes Initiative	Trapped by Inertia
Self-Reliant	Dependent
Self-Motivated	Lack of Motivation
Accept Personal Responsibility	Lack of Personal Responsibility
Abundant Mentality	Scarcity Mentality

Identify your Core Beliefs

Circle which beliefs you know are helping you take the action needed to master this fundamental and critical skill: overcoming objections.

Remember: Trigger Traits—for success or failure—are the outward reflection of your inner core beliefs.

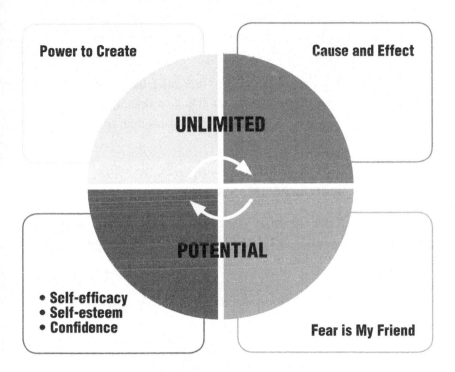

- **Power to Create:** If I cannot see myself, first, as the best, I cannot become the best. All success is created/ envisioned in my mind's eye first.

- **Unlimited Potential:** If I do not believe I can grow, change, adjust and "become," I will not persevere and work tirelessly to master the fundamental skills of my trade. We must believe we can before we will do the things we need to do.

- **Cause & Effect:** If I do not believe that all success is a function of cause and effect, I will focus on the wrong tasks and never consistently execute the right strategies (best practices) essential to my success. As such, I will fail to accept personal responsibility for my results (strong or weak).

- **Self-Efficacy/Self-Esteem:** I must see all feedback in life as not good or bad, but simply information to tap my potential. Otherwise, I will never persevere, remain positive and committed to skill mastery and achievement of my goals.

- **Fear is My Friend:** If I fail to recognize that fear is not my enemy but my friend, I will fail to dream, try new things, and execute on the ideas, plans and strategies needed to succeed.

Action Step: Reflect, Adjust, Succeed

Based upon your identified beliefs and traits, take a moment now to complete your reflection and determine your path forward with the exercise below.

When it comes to the fundamentals/Best Practices needed to master overcoming objections:

I. What Have I Done Right?

II. What Have I Done Wrong?

III. What Will I Do Differently?

Chapter 14:

PROSPECTING: THE PRELUDE TO SALES SUCCESS

> *"You will become lethal in sales by doing the work—seeing the people."*

With the passing of time and my first full year in sales under my belt, I learned more about shaping and refining a Swagger-Set and Selling Skills than most people learn in their first ten years of their sales career, if at all.

I knew for sure the way to the sway of those that become masters of Swagger Selling. Although I cannot say I was a master of the sway just yet, I for sure was well on my way.

But why was it happening for me so fast, and with such precision?

As I sat in reflection—a skill I was very proficient by this point in time—I knew it was for sure because of the careful and strategic teachings of my coach and mentor, Randy.

He coached my every **action**, making sure I was following the best practices of each and every stage of the sales process.

He mentored my current and evolving **beliefs**, making sure that I internalized the five core beliefs that are the pillars to creating a Swagger-Set.

However, none of this would have accelerated my growth if it were not for one simple thing he taught me and helped me to do every single day: Prospect.

That is correct, prospect. Becoming a master prospector enabled me to practice and hone my Swagger-Set and Skill-Set because of the pure volume and consistent practice I was able to capture every single day.

And as I reflected, I laughed out loud because I realized that this all emerged from that first cup of coffee he insisted we get at the student center each and every time we arrived on campus. I really thought we did it primarily to shake off the cold, and secondarily look at our game plan for the day. But as I sat and pondered, I realized it was primarily to shake off any jitters and distractions regarding exactly whom we would meet and sell to that day. Randy helped me to become a master prospector, by constantly reminding me during my first year that I would never perfect what he was teaching me or succeed unless I "saw the people."

1. See the right people: professors using and controlling the adoption (purchase) of the books we sold.
2. Conduct 12 to 15 sales interviews a day to practice and perfect my selling skills and attitudes.

As the man with the Swagger would always say each morning in that student center with a coffee, "Joe, you will become lethal in sales by doing the work—seeing the people. Bunches and bunches of people! Those who rise rapidly to the top do so because they practice too soon and too often rather than too late and not enough."

Swag-Step 1: The Goal of Mastering the Ability to Prospect

To the professional salesperson, there is nothing more precious than a prospect. With an endless bounty of well-qualified prospects, a salesperson of virtually any skill level is destined to reach the pinnacle of sales success and become a master of Swagger Selling. Conversely, without prospects, sales is an uphill battle in which a salesperson struggles to survive.

Swag-Step 2: The Purpose of Prospecting

As Paul J. Meyer, founder of Success Motivation Institute (another man with Swagger I had the honor of getting to know well in my career) eloquently put it, "I would rather be a master prospector than a wizard of speech and have no one to share my story with."

When one truly takes the time to study the business of selling, they quickly learn that all sales success is governed by the laws of statistics. For every "X" number of presentations, you will make "Y" number of sales. While the ratios will vary from salesperson to salesperson depending on their selling attitudes and skill level, as soon as you recognize this phenomenon, you will realize that a salesperson with the ability to prospect cannot fail. And not only can this salesperson not fail, they are destined to become a top producer.

The reason for this is quite simple: Such salespeople spend infinitely more time in the sales arena perfecting their selling skills. Simply put, when it comes to any new skill development, the more time someone spends practicing it, the better they will become. This is true whether a person is attempting to learn how to play the piano, hit a golf ball or become a master salesperson.

Without a doubt, the key to a long and highly prosperous career in sales lies in your ability to prospect. However, given the obvious importance of prospecting, it is surprising to note that very few salespeople consciously strive to master this fundamental and crucial skill. But why? Well, as you know at this point in our journey, most new and even tenured sales professionals are never carefully coached and mentored to create the critical Swagger-Set first! As a result, their lack of discipline needed to follow a sales plan comprised of best practices, the inability to reflect and use every situation as a learning experience, coupled with the debilitating grip of call reluctance fueled by fear, leaves them completely devoid of the mindset needed to master the fundamentals of the sales process.

This critical gap (missing ingredient) in their professional development is the reason that far too many sales professionals among us become the Jack-of-All-Trades and Master of None.

In this final chapter, we will study the best practices and proven strategies that are used by top sales professionals to prospect. In mastering these techniques you, too, will possess the final fundamental selling skill essential to the progressive realization of your dreams.

Swag Step 3: The Best Practices of Master Prospectors

When you stop and truly examine it, there are seven primary methods utilized by master salespeople to engage new sales prospects:

- Referral Introductions
- Center of Influence Introductions
- Nesting
- Past Dormant Customers
- Migrating Decision Makers/Clients
- Personal Observation
- Cold Reach Out, Utilizing Social Media Tools—Specifically LinkedIn

Note: Technology and social media services like email or LinkedIn allow us to approach the list of prospecting techniques above differently today from a mere ten years ago, but these seven methods are still the core fundamentals of prospecting.

On the following pages, we will discuss each of these prospecting methods in order of effectiveness and profitability.

1. Referral Prospecting

If you look at the very top sales producers in your industry or any industry, you will always find men and women who have mastered the ability to referral prospect. There is no doubt that referral prospecting is by far the most powerful technique of finding highly qualified sales leads. Yet, surprisingly, it is the least utilized method. Given the obvious benefits, one is forced to wonder why this is.

Why Do Most Sales Professionals Fail to Master Referral Prospecting?

There are two primary reasons that salespeople fail to get referrals: first, they never earn the right to ask for and receive them, and second and by far the biggest reason, because they simply fail to ask.

Earning the Right to Get Referrals

The key to earning the right to get referrals lies in a salesperson's ability to qualify. At its most fundamental level, sales is all about solving problems. By asking the appropriate probing questions during the qualify, a salesperson is able to diagnose the challenge and isolate its cause, and thereby help the prospect. Only by properly doing this is a salesperson truly able to present an effective solution to the prospect. It is in this process of asking questions, isolating challenges and presenting effective solutions that a salesperson is able to create a significant benefit to the prospect.

By clarifying a prospect's thought process, isolating their challenge and providing them with a workable solution, you provide significant benefits during the sales interview. The more benefits you provide, the more likely they are to give you referrals. By closely following the sales process described throughout this book, you will create what is referred to as a **stroke deficit** with every prospect with whom you conduct a sales interview.

The stroke deficit is a term used to describe one of the most powerful laws of human relations: The Law of Reciprocation. Simply put, the Law of Reciprocation describes that strong urge you feel to help someone who has just helped you. An excellent example of this occurs every day at department stores across the country. We have all had a total stranger hold open the first set of double doors at the entryway. What typically happens next? You immediately feel the urge to rush to the next set of doors just so you can return the favor. Let this common example impress upon you the power behind this basic law of human interaction.

A professionally executed sales interview conducted with each stage of the sales process successfully implemented, strategically creates a stroke deficit with each prospect. This is because an earnest professional/consultative approach to selling revolves around truly helping your prospects identify and achieve goals that are important to them.

A sales interview that is properly conducted illustrates to the prospect that you genuinely care about them. In addition, a properly conducted sales interview helps the prospect identify personal wants and needs, and provides relevant information on how they can be satisfied. As a result of this, even if a prospect chooses not to buy, a well-run sales interview still provides the prospect with immediate benefit, and the internal urge is created to reciprocate.

The challenge is that, in many cases, prospects simply do not know the best way they can reciprocate or repay you for helping them solve their challenges. They do not understand that the best way they can help you is by introducing you to other potential prospects (i.e. giving you referrals). Because most people are not sophisticated in the ways of selling, they don't understand that the most valuable thing a salesperson has is a new prospect. It is a salesperson's responsibility to show the prospect how best to repay or return the favor, which you do by asking for referrals.

Swag-Hint

Never make the cardinal mistake of assuming that a prospect knows that they can return the help you just provided to them through your professional sales interview by providing you with referrals.

You must ASK!

Action Step

Review your entire sales presentation with a critical eye. Are you adequately demonstrating your concern and desire to assist your prospect? Can you provide greater benefit or be of more service during your presentation? Make a list of all the things that you can do to strengthen each stage of the sales process to create this greatest value to them:

1.

2.

3.

4.

5.

6.

7.

8.

9.

10.

How to Ask for and Receive Referrals

Top sales producers leave nothing to chance. They understand the dynamics of human interaction, and they understand that 80% of all communication happens non-verbally. For these reasons, a master salesperson never leaves the most important aspect of their sales call—asking for referrals—to chance. Top sales producers will always end each sales call with a well-rehearsed strategic referral presentation.

A well-developed referral presentation will always consist of two parts. First, the Referral "Introduction," and second, the "Focusing" Question(s). Each of these serves a highly strategic role in securing introductions to well-qualified prospects to sell.

In developing the introduction stage of your referral presentation, you will want to accomplish two significant goals: first, to remind the prospect (diplomatically) of how much you've been able to help them, and second, to establish and define the way that they can reciprocate or repay you for helping them.

A sample Referral "Introduction" may be:

"Jim, it is impossible for me to know everyone like you that is positive, open to new ideas and would really appreciate the value of what we have been discussing today. As such, I was wondering if I could ask for your help today. Jim, who do you know that is like you, positive and really looking to improve/resolve/address XYZ like we did together today?"

The second part, the "Focusing" Question aspect of your referral presentation is designed to accomplish two tasks: first, to channel the prospect's thought process toward giving you introductions to exactly the type of people you want to meet, and second, to assure that you gain introductions to all of the relevant individuals the prospect knows.

A sample "Focusing" Question section might sound like:

- *"Jim, specifically, I work with a lot of department managers. Who do you know who manages their own department?" (Pause and wait for a response)*
- *"Also, I do a lot of work with people in the information technology field. Who do you know that works in information technology?" (Pause and wait for a response)*
- *"Jim, my company also does a lot of work with business owners. Who do you know who owns their own business?" (Pause and wait for a response)*
- *"Many times, I also get calls from purchasing agents and managers. Who do you know who is in a purchasing role?"*
- *"Jim, I'm also looking to do business with ABC Corporation here in town. Do you know anybody who works for them?"*
- *"Jim, is there anybody else you know that you think it would be a good idea for me to meet?"*

The Action Steps on the following pages will provide the guidance needed to develop your own referral presentation using the concepts in this chapter.

Action Step

Take a moment and define the types of people to whom you want to be referred.

1.

2.

3.

4.

5.

6.

7.

8.

9.

10.

Write a referral presentation to use at the end of every sales call. Be sure that the introduction of your referral presentation reminds the prospect of how much you appreciated the opportunity to meet and to be of value to them. Next, develop a series of Focusing Questions that ask specifically for introductions to the type of people you would like to meet (i.e. *"I do a lot of work with CEOs of small and medium-sized companies. Jim, who do you know that is currently running a public or private company?"*)

Advantages of Referral Prospecting

- Highest payoff method of prospecting (statistically at least 7 out of 10 referred prospects will buy).
- Dramatically reduces time required to book appointments (thereby maximizing time selling).
- Makes rapport building and establishing trust and credibility significantly easier. Dramatically increases a salesperson's closing ratio.
- Helps insulate salesperson from market fluctuations and economic conditions.
- Fastest and most effective way to grow a sales business.

Disadvantages of Referral Prospecting

- Requires a more sophisticated approach to the sales process.

2. Centers of Influence

A derivative of referral prospecting is the use of centers of influence as a means to generate a constant flow of new leads. This method consists of nurturing a relationship with an individual who, for one reason or another, has substantial influence over people who are prime candidates for your product or service. In most cases, these centers of influence are clients of yours who already use your product or service. However, it is possible for a Center of Influence to be someone who is not a client, but believes strongly in you and what you are marketing. As such, they are willing to help by providing you with names of new prospects on a regular basis.

Mastering the skill of developing Centers of Influence is the equivalent of having a Ph.D. in referral prospecting. Developing seven to ten centers of influence for your sales business will put you at the top of your field. However, it is important to realize that Centers of Influence are not found or bought—they are developed.

Best Practice/Strategy

The process of developing strong Centers of Influence for your sales business begins with identifying these special people. Although Centers of Influence will, more often than not, be current or past clients of yours, this is not mandatory. It is important to identify that:

- They are individuals whom you genuinely like and who genuinely like you.
- There is true affinity and electricity between the two of you.
- They are typically individuals who have developed a great deal of respect and belief in you and the product or service you market.
- They are individuals with a great deal of personal power themselves and have a strong professional reputation.

Developing and Cultivating Your Centers of Influence

Once you have identified a potential center of influence, you need to devote special time and resources to nurture this relationship. You should begin by seeking out ways to provide extra benefits to these special people. Pay close attention to details such as their birthday, the names of their children and spouse, hobbies, personal interests and anything that may help them with their business. By seeking ways to be of genuine benefit to these people, you constantly fuel the "stroke deficit" on an ongoing basis.

Often, it is helpful to create a special file folder for each of your centers of influence. In this file, you should keep all of the relevant information about this special person. (Most Customer Relationship Management Systems [CRMs] can help you organize this priceless information.)

> ### *Swag-Hint*
>
> *A few words of caution: It is important that both you and your potential center of influence genuinely like one another. In other words, there is genuine electricity between the two of you. You cannot force an evolved and strong person—or any individual, for that matter—to like, believe and/or to want to support you on an ongoing basis. There must be genuine electricity between the two of you that evolves as you build your relationship.*

Action Step

Identify seven to ten people you know who you can begin developing into centers of influence for your business.

1.

2.

3.

4.

5.

6.

7.

8.

Advantages of Centers of Influence Prospecting

- Provides a virtually endless stream of referrals.
- Leverages salesperson's marketing efforts by creating ambassadors out in the field who are constantly looking for sales opportunities.
- Insulates salesperson from market fluctuations and economic conditions.
- It is the absolute key to abundant sales success.

Disadvantages of Centers of Influence Prospecting

- Requires a more sophisticated approach to the sales process.
- Requires time and effort to build and cultivate center of influence relationships.

3. Nesting

Nesting is also a derivative of referral prospecting. Nesting consists of making a sale within a given company, profession, association or group, and then focusing on acquiring the names of other people related to that group. This is an extremely effective and strategic way to grow your sales business, because over time, you become an expert at solving the wants and needs of this target audience. In a short period of time, your ability to generate new leads and close sales within this targeted audience will gain strong momentum.

Best Practice/Strategy

To effectively set in motion a nesting prospecting strategy, you will want do three things:

1. Build a list of ideal prospects (companies and types of individuals) you want to target.
2. Begin to ask for referrals to any employees within your targeted companies. Don't worry that this individual may not be the

ideal prospect for you. More often than not, they will be able to introduce you (from the inside) to your ideal prospect.

3. Begin to do research to see if there is a local chapter of a trade association or group that relates to your ideal type of prospect. For example, if one of your ideal prospects happens to be business executives, perhaps the local Chamber of Commerce has an Executives Group that you can nest into.

Some other great sources of nesting opportunities are:

- Chamber of Commerce
- Local Business Groups
- Trade Associations
- Tip or Referral Clubs
- Charitable Organizations
- Health and/or Country Clubs

Swag-Hint

When looking to nest your way into a specific group of people:

1. Search the Encyclopedia of Associations at galegroup.com for potential organizations. In this reference is a listing of all the associations in the United States, including national, state and regional chapters.

2. Search LinkedIn for possible connections. Join groups and connect with people in your target group based on common ground, like companies they've worked for, people they know, or colleges they attended.

Advantages of Nesting

- Highly effective way to gain referrals.
- Maximizes cross-selling opportunities within companies/clients.
- Allows salesperson to gain tremendous insights and expertise within specific targeted markets.
- Can make the entire sales process easier by leveraging relationships to individuals (i.e. people in same company or association) with very similar wants and needs.

Disadvantages of Nesting

- Salesperson can miss other profitable sales opportunities if they are too heavily focused on a singular market.
- Adverse industry economic situations can have a dramatic negative impact on a salesperson if they are too heavily focused in one vertical industry.

Action Step

Take a moment and remind yourself of the companies and types of people you would like to meet.

Identify four companies you could sell and then nest within.

1.
2.
3.
4.

Pick three groups or types of people with whom you would like to use the nesting strategy.

1.
2.
3.

4. Past Dormant Customers and Migrating Decision Makers/ Clients

If the product or service you are selling is truly of value to the people who have purchased it in the past, these clients become a great source of new business in the future in three ways. First, they themselves may have a need for additional purchases. Second, these happy clients represent a tremendous source of referrals. And third, sometimes key decision makers migrate from one department/division to another or from one company to another. LinkedIn is a powerful way to follow them and harvest new sales opportunities.

It is staggering how many established sales professionals and/or organizations overlook this enormous source of new sales.

Action Step

Make a list of the past customers you can approach this week.

1.	Phone #	Email
2.	Phone #	Email
3.	Phone #	Email
4.	Phone #	Email
5.	Phone #	Email
6.	Phone #	Email
7.	Phone #	Email
8.	Phone #	Email
9.	Phone #	Email
10.	Phone #	Email

Using LinkedIn, look to see which decision makers of the past may have migrated to new departments or even organizations that present new sales opportunities.

Advantages of Prospecting Past Dormant Customers

- Highly effective way to gain qualified prospects.
- Maximizes cross-selling opportunities within companies.
- Can make the entire sales process easier by leveraging previous relationships to other related individuals (i.e. people in same company or association).

Disadvantages of Prospecting Past Dormant Customers

- Salesperson can waste valuable time trying to resuscitate relationships that for one reason or another are just not viable.

5. Personal Observation

Personal observation is a great method of prospecting that you can use to complement your other methods. Many professional salespeople know and use this method effectively. It consists of always keeping a watchful eye out for potential prospects. You will be surprised how many potential prospects you encounter throughout the day. Many salespeople pass by hundreds of potential prospects each year because they meet people outside of the business environment and, therefore, don't look at these people from a sales perspective.

The single biggest key to becoming effective at personal observation is to recognize your goal. When you identify a potential prospect, remember your goal is not to deliver a sales presentation. It is simply to pique the prospect's interest and secure a sales appointment or obtain a phone number and/or email address where you can contact the prospect to arrange a sales appointment at a future time.

Action Step

Take a moment and reflect on the people with whom you interact. Think about those individuals that you have met through social engagements, club memberships, your place of worship, etc. Who among these people would be good prospects? Who among these people work for companies with which you would like to do business? Who among these people could refer you to good sales prospects? Make a list of all the people with whom you intend to follow-up.

1.
2.
3.
4.
5.
6.
7.
8.
9.
10.
11.
12.
13.
14.
15.

Advantages of Personal Observation

- Easy method of finding sales leads.
- Can allow for wide diversity in prospects/companies.

Disadvantages of Personal Observation

- Given no previous relationship with prospect, it can be harder to establish trust and credibility.
- Requires salesperson to stay outside of their comfort zone and have their "sales hat" on 24 hours a day.

6. The Cold Reach-Out (once known simply as "The Cold Call")

The cold call, or reach-out, as we label it today, is still among the most popular and commonly used method of prospecting with salespeople. However, this method has always been the least effective means of finding new prospects. This has been particularly compounded by technology—specifically, the advent of caller ID, voicemail and the heavy shift to the utilization of cell phones rather than office phones. The professional and strategic salesperson knows that the infamous cold call has its place, but only under two circumstances:

1. If you are establishing a new territory for your company where neither you nor your company has had any prior contact.
2. If you attempt to enter a new industry or field with your product or service and have no prior experience or contacts. In both cases, the cold reach-out would be necessary until you can begin to utilize other, more effective methods of prospecting discussed earlier. Once you have made some initial contacts and begin conducting sales interviews, referral prospecting should prevail.

Nonetheless, there are three techniques that will increase the effectiveness of your cold reach-out efforts:

1. Find and use optimal lead sources that are comprised of the decision makers you seek.
2. Use a pre-approach email.
3. Maintain a positive attitude.

A. Find and Use Optimal Lead Sources

A great way to get cold reach-out leads is to purchase them through a list brokerage house. For example, if you are marketing to advertising executives, it is very likely that you will be able to buy a comprehensive list of executives in the advertising industry.

> ### *Swag-Hint*
>
> *When purchasing lists, be sure to ask how recently the information on the list has been updated. If a list is too old or outdated, more than likely, the information will no longer be relevant. Many list companies will also guarantee the accuracy of the information, so be sure to ask for a guarantee.*

> ### *Swag-Hint*
>
> *When looking for a list of contacts within a specific group, try "The Book of Lists." This is a comprehensive guide to all of the contact lists and databases that are available for purchase. You can find this as a database at:*
> *http:/ www.bizjournals.com/bizbooks*

B. Using a Pre-Approach Letter

In many cases, using a pre-approach letter can pave the way for improved results with follow-on calls. This is because a well-written letter can pique the interest of a decision maker and introduce you to them prior to you making the call.

> ### *Swag-Hint*
>
> *If you plan to use a pre-approach letter, be sure to plan and allocate the time to make the follow-up calls. I am amazed how often I receive a strong letter telling me someone will also call me, and they never do.*

Years ago, I met a crafty sales talent in the health insurance industry who used the pre-approach letter with a unique and powerful twist. He wrote the letter and then crumpled it up in a ball before flattening it back out and placing it in an envelope. The letter opened with the following line: "Dear [NAME], I thought I would save you the time of crumpling up this letter before you toss it in your pail. I was wondering…" The letter is designed to catch the attention of the recipient—which it surely does—and make them laugh and read the rest. This pre-letter technique resulted in the prospect not only taking his follow-up call, but scheduling a sales meeting that resulted in the largest sales in the company's history.

Before you pick up the phone, take a moment to reflect on the success stories of your product/service. Think about how that product/service has been of benefit to the people who have purchased it. Then pick up the phone and speak with confidence, conviction and a true belief that you and your product will dramatically help those people.

Advantages of the Cold Reach-Out

- Salesperson can start booking appointments from day one.
- Good prospecting method for brand new salespeople who have no contacts and relationships that they can otherwise leverage.

Disadvantages of the Cold Reach-Out

- Extremely time consuming. (It can take 30 or more phone calls and/or emails to book one appointment.) Salesperson must face a lot of rejection. This can lead to low morale, lack of motivation/initiative and potentially even turnover.
- Higher appointment cancellation rate.
- Harder to establish trust and credibility with cold leads.
- Salespeople may find themselves spending a lot of prime selling time with bad prospects and non-decision makers.

How to Classify Your Prospects

As your ability to generate new leads improves, you will find that you have more prospects to contact than you have hours in a day. Without implementing a prospect classification and management strategy, you will waste valuable sales time with poor prospects.

The prospect classification strategy below is easy to understand and will ensure that you focus the majority of your sales time speaking with quality prospects. The implementation of this strategy consists of assigning each new prospect a numerical classification as follows:

Classification #1: Those prospects you obtain which have the following attributes: A) The person who provided the referral has a lot of influence over the new prospect (they are the prospect's boss, parent, spouse, sibling or close friend). B) You have obtained pertinent information about the prospect that enables you to conduct a thorough interview (age, occupation, income, marital status, hobbies or any other pertinent information). C) The prospect has a genuine and inherent need for the product/service you are marketing and is the decision maker.

Classification #2: This is a lead where you are given pertinent information about the prospect. The referent even shows you that the prospect has a genuine need for your product/service. However, the referent has little or no influence over the new lead.

Classification #3: A "Class 3" rating should be given to all prospects you have obtained from a source that: A) Has no influence over the new prospect. B) You are unable to obtain any pertinent information about the prospect. C) It is not clear whether or not the prospect has a genuine need for your product/service.

For example, all prospects you obtain through cold reach-out are considered "Class 3" prospects.

How to Organize Your Prospects and Sales Activities

As your sales career continues to ascend, you will begin to find it more and more challenging to keep both your prospects and future sales activities organized. Too often, with an increasingly busy daily schedule, important follow-up calls and sales leads can fall through the cracks. Of course, this represents lost income to both you and your company.

To assure that they don't miss out on potential sales opportunities, top sales producers frequently rely on a Contact Management System. These invaluable tools vary in sophistication from a basic data gathering system to a more comprehensive software application system that combine virtually every aspect of how a salesperson manages their day.

Benefits of using a Contact Management System

- Provides a single source of information on a prospect or client
- Allows you to gather and add additional client/prospect information over time
- Provides a reminder of critical dates for follow-up
- Allows you to monitor where a client/prospect is in the sales cycle
- Creates a more accurate basis for forecasting future sales
- Keeps a dedicated record of information needed for cross-selling or upselling an account
- Makes sales reporting easier
- Assures you never lose or overlook a valuable lead

Regardless of the system you utilize, always remember that the most valuable asset a salesperson possesses is prospects. These prospects represent opportunity to you. They are your future, your success and ultimately the realization of your dreams and desires. As such, every time a prospect gets lost, a lead is overlooked or a follow-up call is missed, potential income is falling out of your pocket. Leveraging a contact management system will help assure that you are capitalizing on all of your opportunities.

A Final Word on Prospecting

The art of prospecting is more than randomly seeking people to whom you can make a presentation. The art of prospecting is mastered by applying the strategic referral skills (and the derivative strategies) we have described and combining them with an effective classification strategy and contact management system.

By mastering these concepts, you control every aspect of your sales business. As an effective, strategic prospector, you decide with whom you want to do business. You paint the picture of your sales destiny as you Swagger your way to the top.

Action Step

Using the various methods of prospecting discussed in this lesson, choose three methods you will begin to use on a' regular basis to generate new business.

1.
2.
3.

A Summary of Swagger Fundamentals for Prospecting

- Prospecting is the key to sales success.
- An abundance of prospects allows you to continually refine and master the sales skills you need to succeed.
- The most valuable method of prospecting is referrals.
- Developing "Centers of Influence" is the key to endless sales leads.
- Nesting is an extremely effective and strategic way to grow your sales business within a target audience.
- Engage dormant past customers.
- Follow migrating decision makers or clients through technology such as LinkedIn.
- Cold call potential leads and use pre-approach letters when no other means of prospecting are an option within a new market.
- Classify your prospects in order of priority.

Swag-Step 4: The Swagger-Set Diagnostic Tool

The Power of Reflection

Only by truly establishing where you are now, can you crystallize your path forward to total sales mastery.

Identify your Trigger Traits

When it comes to your efforts so far to refine and master the fundamental and critical skill of prospecting, which words best describe your behavior? (circle all that apply)

Trigger Traits of Success ↑ Swagger-Set (Optimal Core Beliefs)	Trigger Traits of Failure ↑ No-Swagger (Limiting Beliefs)
Creative	Indifferent
Imaginative	Unimaginative
Positive	Negative
Persistent	Easily Discouraged
Resilient	Defeatist
Adaptive	Inability to Adapt/Change and Grow
Determined	Wavering
Courageous	Fearful
Confident	Lack of Confidence
Takes Initiative	Trapped by Inertia
Self-Reliant	Dependent
Self-Motivated	Lack of Motivation
Accept Personal Responsibility	Lack of Personal Responsibility
Abundant Mentality	Scarcity Mentality

Identify your Core Beliefs

Circle which beliefs you know are helping you take the action needed to master this fundamental and critical skill: prospecting.

Remember: Trigger Traits—for success or failure—are the outward reflection of your inner core beliefs.

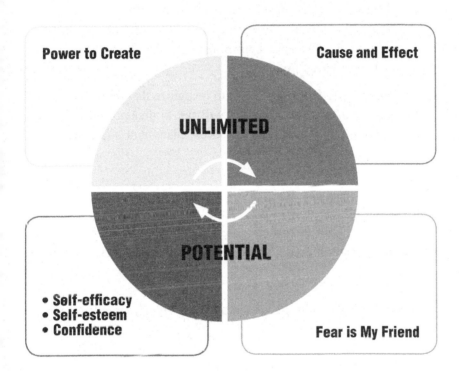

- **Power to Create:** If I cannot see myself, first, as the best, I cannot become the best. All success is created/envisioned in my mind's eye first.

- **Unlimited Potential:** If I do not believe I can grow, change, adjust and "become," I will not persevere and work tirelessly to master the fundamental skills of my trade. We must believe we can before we will do the things we need to do.

- **Cause & Effect:** If I do not believe that all success is a function of cause and effect, I will focus on the wrong tasks and never consistently execute the right strategies (best practices) essential to my success. As such, I will fail to accept personal responsibility for my results (strong or weak).

- **Self-Efficacy/Self-Esteem:** I must see all feedback in life as not good or bad, but simply information to tap my potential. Otherwise, I will never persevere, remain positive and committed to skill mastery and achievement of my goals.

- **Fear is My Friend:** If I fail to recognize that fear is not my enemy but my friend, I will fail to dream, try new things, and execute on the ideas, plans and strategies needed to succeed.

Action Step: Reflect, Adjust, Succeed

Based upon your identified beliefs and traits, take a moment now to complete your reflection and determine your path forward with the exercise below.

When it comes to the fundamentals/Best Practices needed to master prospecting:

I. What Have I Done Right?

II. What Have I Done Wrong?

III. What Will I Do Differently?

Epilogue:

THE REASON WHY

Epilogue:

THE REASON WHY

How do you repay someone that taught you how to become the best you can be at anything you choose to do in life; a leader who took the time and care to teach you how to Swagger and apply the "way of the sway" to live the career and life you coveted in your heart since adolescence and as a young adult?

The answer, quite frankly is you can't; and what I have come to learn is that those who take the time to teach others to live their life with Swagger want nothing more than the returned gift of honor and respect.

Honor, meaning that once we discover how to build and live our life with Swagger, we will apply it with reverence to become the best we can be—not just in sales—but in every aspect of our life!

Respect, in that those that embrace and master the power of Swagger will respect its application and share it with others "to make good"—wherever your life's journey leads you.

Approximately 26 plus years after learning how to Swagger Sell and Live, I was blessed with the opportunity to meet up with several of my colleagues from that magical sales team my mentor had graciously invited me to join all those years ago. Each of us shared how the very trajectory of our lives had been profoundly and positively altered because of what our mutual friend, teacher and mentor took the time to bequeath to us. Beth, went on to start her own publishing company and achieve tremendous heights in her career; Caroline, took her talent to the Pharmaceutical industry where she quickly rose to be a Top Producing Sales Representative before retiring early to raise her children. We were all direct benefactors of the same insights and specialized knowledge revealed to you throughout this manuscript.

For over 25 years, I have been blessed to work side-by-side with 2logical's extraordinary Executives, specifically Co-founder/VP David Naylor and VP and Director of Global Training John Casey, along with an incredible team of dedicated associates, client leaders and friends teaching tens of thousands of people the "way of the sway" to reach their full potential in sales and in life.

Whether it be our friends from the East Coast to the West Coast and every state in between, as well as our neighbors in Canada and Mexico, or those dancing in Central/South America, the Middle East, Asia and the Pacific Rim; everyone wants to learn the Swagger Sway!

As my friend, John Casey, always reminds me from his global travels, "People the world over want one dominant thing: to live a successful life and raise their children to do the same."

I am both proud and humbled by the positive results we have been able to help people achieve throughout the world by showing them the steps to live and sell with Swagger.

Together, this formula has placed struggling billion dollar sales companies back onto the path of greatness—striking great fear into their competition along the way from the power of the sway. It has been credited with sparing countless newly minted sales professionals from the perils of despair and certain failure, by showing them the path and teaching them the steps to Swagger (Swagger-Set + Fundamental Skill-Set = Results). It has enabled tenured sales professionals to leave behind the lethargy that has shackled them to mediocrity and become a peak performer, financially independent and enabled them to join the ranks of the "sales elite"—the stature captured by all those that sell with Swagger.

As I write these final words to you, I am reminded of a sales call with a top Executive at a global company I was selling to years ago. It is one story of the literal thousand I could share just like it.

As I sat and built Rapport with this bright, energetic executive, completed my Transitional Success Story to break any preoccupation and draw him into the discussion at hand, I began my Qualify which was quickly greeted with:

"Joe, I am a believer in training and I am so glad you are here...you see, I have a very seasoned and tenured sales force, and what we need is some advanced sales training!" he exclaimed. "We need advanced training to salvage my struggling performers, help my mid-level performers and inspire my best producers."

"Really?" I said, with the calm of a ninja who has already won the war. "That is interesting Stan, but I was wondering if I could ask you a brief question or two."

"Sure!" he quipped back with a big, radiant smile, "What would you like to know?"

"Well, I'm just curious, who on your sales team (the average tenure was over ten years) is lethal at the fundamental skills of selling? Lethal at:
- Rapport
- Transitional Success Stories
- Qualifying
- Presentations
- Closing
- Overcoming Objections
- and Prospecting?"

He paused for a moment in reflection as his eyes lifted upward and then slowly said, "Well, B-B-B-Bonnie in Baltimore, she is pretty good..." as he slowly released the name that was marbled up in his mouth.

I then politely said, "Well that is insightful Stan, but I did not ask who is pretty good, I asked who are the men and women on your team that are lethal at the fundamentals, meaning they have complete and utter mastery of the basics of our trade—selling?"

As Stan pondered, he turned his head slowly to look out the window, and then turned back and reflectively said, "You know Joe, I really can't name anyone among my tenured sales team that is a true master of the fundamentals...but I never thought about it quite like this before."

As Stan started to drift in thought, I caught him from a mental free fall with a simple statement and a follow-up question:

"Stan, the best athletes in the world are masters of the fundamentals, the best armies in the world are masters of the fundamentals, and so are the best painters, musicians, chefs and virtually any other vocation you can possibly think of.

"Why do you think so few ever master the fundamentals of our trade and reach the pinnacle of sales success?" I softly inquired.

He replied, "I-I'm not really sure...We absolutely provide everyone on the sales team with fundamental sales skill/ process training...I don't actually know."

Stan did not know the reason why; **but you surely do now...Swagger!**

Appendix A:

SWAGGER STORIES

Appendix A

SWAGGER STORIES

It is my honor to share just a few of the thousands of stories of astounding success from the countless sales professionals that we have helped to master the "way of the sway." Their legacies are a testament to the pure power and infinite potential of a human being determined to succeed.

Betsy
Top Health Insurance Company

The Office Receptionist that Became the #1 Sales Person

I thought that this was an appropriate time to express my appreciation for all you have given me. **From the time when we first met until today, your knowledge and guidance has been instrumental in every decision that I have made.**

When we first met, I was an administrator, perfectly content, or so I believed, to be a "behind the scenes" person. **At that point in time, I had ABSOLUTELY no desire to be in a sales position.** This belief slowly started to change as you made me see that, even though I wasn't in outside sales, to my internal customers, I had to sell myself and my abilities or end up being another nine to five drone. It was my choice. It changed the way I interacted with all of the people that I was dealing with on a daily basis.

The shift in attitude continued when I was promoted to a Service Representative. I was in my element! Taking care of my clients' needs and building relationships that continue through today. You showed me that I was still selling myself, this time on an even higher level. I was able to troubleshoot problems and get results, which resulted in my clients' confidence in my abilities. They knew who to call when an issue arose. However, at that point in time, I still had no real desire to be in a "real" sales position, even though I knew that was where you were leading me (kicking and screaming). **You, with great patience I might add, finally made me realize that if I wanted to progress in my career, that I would seriously have to expand my comfort zones.**

Expand my comfort zones indeed. **You taught me step-by-step what I needed to be "the best of the best."** At that time you had infinitely more confidence in my abilities that I did. You had to overcome my weaknesses, as well as my doubts. Well my friend, I am happy to say that you succeeded! **We succeeded, beyond anything that I had ever imagined.**

I know that I have much more that I can learn from you and I sincerely look forward to our continuing meetings. **Hey, now that I have the basics down, just imagine what else I can do with more of your training sessions!**

Sincerely,

Betsy W.

PS. Boomer and the Miss America Pageant? The mind boggles!

Life with Swagger

The day I met Betsy, she was the receptionist of the Cincinnati sales office for this iconic health care company. She made obscene hand signals behind my back as she walked me down the hall to meet the regional sales vice president...that is until I stopped short in the hall, and she crashed into me.

I then said, "I like your moxie. I am going to make sure you are included in the sales training I will be implementing here next week."

Betsy ultimately—after several prior promotions (administrator to customer service representative to sales representative)—became the #1 sales representative in the company.

Pete

Top 5 Insurance Company

The Sales Manager Who Did the Impossible

It seems as if it were only yesterday when I was first introduced to you. I must admit that I was rather receptive to meeting you back then since I was new to the Rochester community and desperately needed to fill my appointment book.

When I think back to that time, however, I now recognize my total naiveté in thinking that the Rochester agency employed only seventeen associates and was capable of a mere $490,000 totally first year commissions. **Equally discouraging, many industry professionals warned that a Rochester agency could no longer grow demographically, or profitably.** You immediately allayed my apprehension in our initial meeting as the synergy, passion and energy developed and flourished between us. **Truly, all great players are taught by great coaches, and you are mine.**

Within a mere fifteen months, we 'knocked the cover off the ball' by recruiting seventy agents and completing last year with $1.2 million FYC. This was no fluke as the Rochester agency will conclude this year with $1.3 million FYC. In addition, I have won every possible award and like Rick Pitino, I have accepted a new challenge; rebuilding the "flagship" agency of our firm. I realize that without your encoring efforts and continued guidance, this opportunity never would have presented itself.

Thank you and I look forward to continuing our work together for many years to come.

Sincerely,

Pete

Life with Swagger

The world moves aside for people who commit and follow the path to becoming the very best! In his new assignment, Pete went on to lead the flagship agency of the firm to great new heights.

Gregg
Automotive

The #1 Service Advisor

I am writing you this letter to let you know how much your training has done for me both personally and professionally. **Your training has taught me the skills necessary to advance myself to levels I thought were not possible before.**

My main achievements have come professionally and they involve becoming the #1 Service Advisor for Buick Motors division in the nation. I have no doubt that the main reason I was able to achieve this was due to your training, which lead to my realization that I have unlimited potential. **With the help and resources you have given me, I know that this is only the beginning of things to come.**

Thanks again for everything. I know I will see you in the future, hopefully at the top.

Sincerely,

Gregg E.

Life with Swagger

Gregg, after recognizing and learning how to harness his potential, ripped the lid off of his career and become the #1 service advisor in the United States.

Mark
Top 5 Insurance Company

The Good Salesperson That Became Great

Thank you for the help that you have extended to me. **I don't think many people really know what you are doing for them in their lives.** I hope the organization does as it is my belief what you are working for can only take everyone to new success if they want it.

When we started, I felt that I was already a good salesperson. I was doing very well in the organization and saw things for what they were. The focus being selling and servicing my clients. I have always had drive and a competitive spirit and I think you put it best: *"You are good but you can be better."* I know that is true for me and anyone else out there in the world. It does not matter if you are the best, you can always be better, as a salesperson and as a human being.

What I don't think people realize is that when you become a better person you elevate yourself to a new level. This is what I think is the greatest lesson that I am learning. I am seeing new perspectives that I think will take me to new possibilities in my personal life as well as professional life.

I am seeing and practicing the techniques you have shown me. Finding the prospects, organizing them, qualifying them, and pursuing them has always been there for me. What I see is the depth that I am focusing on to make my plan more effective. Working on the referrals, contacts, and centers of influence to open the doors of abundance for me. Bringing out the best of my relationship building skills in order to influence that cold call has brought new successes for me. I have always felt the ability, you are taking that and giving me a gift, a free tune-up that lasts a lifetime.

This last week with you is when I saw the area that I can really develop, the presentation. I feel I have all the abilities, but what I did see is that I can become more effective in controlling the situation. Leading the client down the path to a sale is what I enjoy most and your suggestions of looking at each chamber of a sales call hit home with me. I am excited to bring this art to a new level. I know having you there to critique me, notice each chamber and to work together has had an impact.

As I look at where I am going and my goals, I know that I am developing myself as the best salesperson I can be and more. I want to grow and I have seen results from your instruction just in simple things like working with my team and crystallizing for them their goals. The same thing we have done I believe has resulted in better performance out of my people. I know that my personal development is going to produce results not only in my sales but also influence others to reach their goals and objectives.

I have gone through many courses but to me, your help you cannot put a price on. The organization needs a sales mentor focused on the people. I know you have extended yourself to me, and given the choice to take or leave your knowledge, it is not a question to me. I truly believe that you have had a great impact on me and I appreciate it.

Let me know if there is anything that I can do for you.

Sincerely,

Mark C.

Life with Swagger

Mark received an offer to become the Regional Vice President of his insurance company. He sent me this letter a little over 3 years later:

Dear Joe,

I wanted to take a minute of your time and say hello. It has been awhile but funny as it may sound seems like yesterday when we were working together.

As the year came and went, I look back and cannot help see what I planned for, and set me goals for and what I am going to bring for myself in 1998. At the same time I can't help but think of you and what you have given to me and many others.

Joe, I had one of my best years ever (127% of goal) and more importantly have never been happier in my personal and professional life I know this can be attributed to our time together, your effort and I wanted you to know your training has played a big role in my life success.

I hope all is well with you and your family and if you ever need anything just let me know.

Sincerely,

Mark

John
Top 5 Property and Casualty Insurance Company

The #1 Producing Agent

Becoming the number one producing agent out of the 500 agents in my region is just one of the many goals I have achieved. Enhancing my abilities to generate referred leads and develop strong centers of influence in my marketplace has not only enabled me to significantly increase my income, it has enabled me to do so without having to commit any additional hours to work each day.

As you have often said, "Working hard is not enough. If you are going to rise to the top of your field and live a balanced life, we must commit to working smart."

Over the years, I have retained your company's services many times. Each time it has inspired me to continue to work hard, while providing me with the knowledge to work smart. I sincerely appreciate the support you have given through the years and the friendship that has grown. I look forward to the years ahead with positive expectancy.

Sincerely,

John B.

Life with Swagger

As John mentions, he went on to sway his way to the top, becoming the #1 agent in his region, out of 500 peers. John has consistently achieved his goals and set records throughout the years of his career.

Ken
Top 5 Oil Services Company

The Transformation of Experienced Sales Leaders

I want to thank you for the experience of a lifetime. Going into the class, I was skeptical and prepared for it to be a waste of time. I was actually hoping that a "fire" would crop up somewhere, and I would be required to step out and help put it out, and possibly get out of class. **By the end of Day 1, I realized that this class was like no other.** I was amazed as I watched the class transform in just a few days—and these are successful, experienced sales leaders within our organization—and the way they view their jobs was changed in a very short amount of time. My mind was changed as well, and I have begun a new journey in my life which I am looking at not as a new chapter, but a new volume in my professional and personal life. **I have already found myself using the techniques we learned last week,** and I look forward to tomorrow when I can continue developing into a better leader while helping our company and other people grow.

A quick story—since the first of the year, I have lost about 40 lbs. (Yes, playing soccer with 40 less pounds is easier!). As you could imagine, the clothes I wore before don't fit me anymore, and I ended up stacking them in a corner of our bedroom. My wife has asked me many times what I was going to do with my "big clothes." I told her I didn't know, but in my mind, I was keeping them in case I needed them again. I woke up this morning, stuffed them in a bag, and gave them away to Goodwill. My wife asked me why I decided to get rid of them now. I simply told her that I don't need them anymore.

Thank you!

Ken M.

Life with Swagger

Ken's application of the specialized knowledge he received from my close friend and associate, John Casey, has consistently fueled his professional and personal success to new heights.

Stephen
Regional Financial Services Company

From Skeptic to Believer

I am writing you this letter to express my sincerest appreciation toward you and your program. Being in the financial industry, I have been exposed to a lot of sales classes that promise you the world but never deliver. When I started your class, I was a bit of a skeptic, however, over a short period of time I began to realize that your approach was very different. It took into consideration my strengths and weaknesses and taught me how to become better at everything I do.

Over the last year my sales have increased more than 120% and this year proves to be even better. Referrals are starting to flow to me easily, up 50% from last year, and my personal life is also making great strides. I am happily married and look forward to each and every day with great enthusiasm. Your guidance has exposed a world full of great potential for me.

Thank you for not only being a great mentor, but also a true friend.

Sincerely,

Stephen

Life with Swagger

As a new entry into our world of "professional selling," Steve has gone on to build an illustrious career in sales!

Bill

International Technology Services Company

The Sales Renaissance of a 40 Year Old Company

October 31st marked our year-end and also marked the first full business year of our relationship with 2logical and yourself. The results are in and we've had our finest sales performance in the history of our company (over 40 years). We have increased our sales from last year over 15%. This is the first time we had an increase in the past ten years. I can say unequivocally that you have made a tremendous impact on those results.

The consistent training and coaching has given us the knowledge and awareness of how we can achieve our dreams and goals. This not only applies to our business and endeavors, but also has affected our personal lives as well.

With the foundation firmly in place, next year will again prove to be our most successful year. We are now poised to grow and expand to fulfill our business and professional goals as well as our personal goals.

Thanks for all your help this year—looking forward to a successful next year!

Very truly yours,

Bill

Life with Swagger

Bill and his dynamic team have retained my firm for over 20 years and have never missed a monthly coaching/training meeting—ever. They have built their company into an international powerhouse in their niche market!

James
Leading National Life Insurance Company

The Top 50 Club Member

I would like to take this opportunity to say "thank you" for the professional help you have given me over the past 20 months. You know in a very short time my goals and my dreams have become reality and just recently I qualified for a very high company and personal honor—"Top 50" Club.

Each and every day you have helped me believe in myself and in my business and personal planning. Without these tools that you have given me, I would still be an average person in this business.

Once again, thank you for your personal and professional approach.

Sincerely,

James

Life with Swagger

As he notes, Jim achieved his professional goal of the "Top 50" Club and countless other professional and meaningful personal goals before his work was through. I am humbled that I was able to play a small role in his success and happiness before he departed. May he rest in peace for eternity.

Scott
Regional Health Insurance Company

The #1 Sales Force

I wanted to thank you for the impact that 2logical has made on IH. As the Director of Sales Staff Development and Training, I have been challenged to create a comprehensive training program, that will incorporate all facets of the sales process, ranging from the product training, prospecting, the sales process, creation of a mentoring program, and to change the way our leadership team coaches their team members.

I was with Pfizer for over 20 years and was a Senior District Manager for over 17 years. Pfizer's training has always been considered the best in the industry. Most recently over the last 2 years, I was the Director of Sales for BlueCross BlueShield of Western New York. In the last 22 years, I have had the opportunity to participate in a variety of training programs and outside consultants. This is the best training program that I have ever participated in. IH has worked with a number of vendors, but as I was told, the majority of these training companies were not impactful or considered the "flavor of the month." **It is nice to know that IH has been so impressed with this training, and that for the first time, 2logical is not considered a flavor of the month, but rather a partner that we will working with for years to come.** I have both the Leadership and Sales teams asking when our next Builder Meeting will be. We also plan to have your organization participate in our corporate kickoff meeting in September, of which our organization has never had an outside vendor attend. **I appreciate the fact that your company tailors the training to the needs of our company, rather than a training program off the shelf.** Your trainer's ability to take the different concepts and relate them to companies he has dealt with throughout the world as well as relate them to IH was incredible.

With the extensive amount of internal training that is being rolled out, by having 2logical involved early in the process has created a culture that has turned the Leadership and Sales team around. I have seen a change in both attitude as well as the focus on High Payoff Activities.

Initially, IH was ranked last in our market. Because of the impact that 2logical had with a shift in mindset and beliefs, the team has, within the first year, moved to number two, and by the second year, moved to number one.

Thank you so much for the impact that your company has already had on IH, and truly look forward to our continued partnership. I am a true believer that the best is yet to come, and with your company's assistance, we will be able to achieve market dominance.

With the challenges that exist in the marketplace today, the training 2logical provides will help differentiate our company from our competitors.

Regards,

Scott

Life with Swagger

Before learning the "way of the sway," IH's sales force was ranked last in the region. In the first year, the sales force shot up to #2, and by the second year, the sales force secured the #1 spot. As of the printing of this manuscript, they are still #1.

Marc
Global Technology Company

Impacting Multi-National Corporations

Excerpt from video testimonial

The fundamental difference that makes 2logical different from any other training organization is their approach because their approach very much focuses on the mindset and the belief structure of the individuals within an organization. Before you get to more of the skill-set and tactical elements of how to be successful as an individual you have to focus on mindset and belief structure. To me, 2logical taking the approach that everything starts there fundamentally and nothing else can be impacted until you get the person in the right mindset and belief structure, that is the element that makes their training different than any other training company in the market.

The impact that 2logical has had on our organization has been truly profound; there's no other way to say it. We were very much an organization before 2logical that was focused on what I would call more the tactical elements of running an organization - activities that our account managers would be doing with the channel partners, focusing on number of activities, focusing on what is the right revenue, what do the sales look like - and all of that is important. I think any business understands that focusing on those elements is critical, but what we really needed as an organization is we had to fundamentally change the culture and the mindset and the belief structure of our organization in order to get our people focused on ultimately, what are the things that needed to be changed in order to impact those numbers.

After partnering with 2logical, we went through a series of trainings with them from our executive leadership staff to our mid-level management staff to our account management staff, feet on the street, even into the fabric of our engineering staff and our accounting department, operations department. What we've seen here in this fiscal year, I can speak for my sales team, we've seen over a 27% increase in our sales year over year from 2014 to 2015, and I think that is very much doing large part to 2logical helping us put our people in the right mindset and belief structure to impact their business. It is a completely different organization than it was a little over a year ago.

2logical's impact on me personally has been profound. I would not be where I am today without their training, just very plain and simple.

Through my experience with Konica Minolta and now with this organization, I've obviously been engaged with 2logical at some level for more than 15 years now. I've really seen it have a profound impact on individuals, obviously it has a profound impact on teams, and it has a profound impact on organizations as a whole.

But as a leader, watching the impact that it has on my team members is truly rewarding and profound. I can think of numerous scenarios where I have team members who are doing things that they would not have done before 2logical training, personally, professionally—setting goals and, not just achieving those goals, but knocking the cover off the ball.

It's like a gift you have and you just want to give it to somebody else to see them be able to grow as well. You know, to me, it's impacted me profoundly but the most rewarding part of it is watching how 2logical can impact other people.

Having already had training with 2logical from Konica Minolta, I was able to come here with the understanding that any organization can ultimately change if given the right information and the right tools in order to make that change.

I scratch my head sometimes and wonder, why aren't more people doing this?

Life with Swagger

Having first experienced and benefited from the unique sales training Marc received at Konica Minolta, Marc knew the tenants of Swagger training was the key to future success…Through the help and guidance of my close friend and associate, Dave Naylor, this organization too has mastered the "way of the sway!"

John

National Life Insurance Company

The Burning for More

In appreciation of all that you've done for me, I've decided to take a minute to sit down and write you this letter.

Over the years, I feel I've been relatively successful, and even though I've accomplished substantially more professionally than my friends and peers of my same age, I've always had a burning feeling that I was missing out on opportunities that were within reach. I met you in May of 1987, and after working with you for six months, I know now why I had that burning feeling. I was not focused, I did not have a clear vision of exactly what it was I wanted, why I wanted it, or specifically how to achieve it.

Today, because of my association with you, Joe, I have a crystal clear picture of where I'm headed, and why I'm headed in that direction. Because of that, I've been able to achieve more in 1987 than I've ever dreamed possible. My unit's production increased by 147%. My personal production increased by 53%. My goal for 1988 is to be the number one sales manager in the company, and for the first time in my life, I know that this is attainable. We all have a tremendous amount of potential and I'm convinced today that those who achieve more than others simply have a clearer vision, and take action.

I can't thank you enough for all that you've done for me in 1987, and I look forward to many years of friendship and a very prosperous business association.

Sincerely,

John

Life with Swagger

John and I have been friends and business associates for over 30 years. Perhaps one of my fondest memories is the lunch we shared about halfway through our journey where we popped a bottle of wine to celebrate his personal achievement of financial independence.

Ken
Regional Mortgage Banking Firm

Monumental Increases

Excerpt from video testimonial

I can say 80% of our sales people this year have had just monumental increases and it is no doubt what the trainings have taught us.

The mindset is the most important part of driving the skills and activities but if you don't have the mindset you can't accomplish it and that is what 2logical has taught us and teaches us from the first day you walk through the door with our firm.

We constantly work with them on their internal side first; we had measured successes that we have seen from new people, veteran people and people that have been with us a couple of years that have exceeded their goals and have done their personal best ever and we have to attribute this to everything we've learned through 2logical's training.

I think giving skills training carte blanche to an organization is a total waste of time. If people don't believe it they won't do it. But if you get them to have the belief and have the right positive mental attitude they will figure it out, yes, you need to show them how to put A in here and B with C and etc., but if you train a group of people that do not have the mindset to have the belief in it or even want it they won't learn it.

So you can do training, training, training and it's not going to change your people's results, it's just going to give them stuff, and stuff is not what drives results. It's the individual's mindset, the individual's drive, the individual's desire that drives that. I would rather have everyone filled with that first, then I can do a skills training, but the skills training does not take the place of your belief in getting it done.

I can have a football team that practices, and practices the same thing, same thing. If they look across the line at the other guys and say, "We'll never beat them," it doesn't matter what they practiced.

How I would describe what 2logical has done for myself, our managers and the management team, I just see continual steady growth. I've got people that have had tremendous years of experience at various institutions, and I have to honestly say, I believe they've excelled under our teaching and the learning that we've had from 2logical. I feel that they've had more success with us, and not just a business success, but a life success. It's transformed me. I couldn't do what I did by building my team, and I can see the progression of people; how they are at the beginning of the year at the end of the year, within 2 years, within 3 years. It's just the transformation has been huge in them being not only a better manager, a better leader, but a better person.

2logical's training personally, for myself, I can't even begin to measure what that is because it's been so valuable to me. It has helped me look at myself and make myself better, it's helped me be a better father, a better husband and a better person, and a person that gives back, and a person that really drives to help people succeed.

When I talk to people, it's not about the numbers, but about helping them find out what they want; because if I help them find out what they want, they're going to drive their numbers, and the numbers are going to be driven to help the company. That's what 2logical has taught me—to have deeper, high trust relationships with people and to really help people achieve.

Life with Swagger

Ken has captured the hearts and minds of all those who have had the pleasure to work with him. Ken understands the power of developing a Swagger-set prior to selling skill-sets. His long record of leading others to unprecedented success is a testament to the "way of the sway."

Marc
Top 5 Oil Services Company

The Salesperson with the Unfair Advantage

Excerpt from video testimonial

What's really unique about the 2logical training is the fact that they really hone in and focus on the thoughts and beliefs, because that's what drives everyone. It drives you in the morning, it drives me in the morning, and that approach is so refreshing because when you sit through a course, you're not just sitting through another management course. You're sitting through a course that, for the most part, you're thinking about yourself first. You're thinking about you as a person and how you can kind of evolve and become better. It's how you think about the scenarios of your work place, it's how you think about scenarios at home. When you realize that your thoughts and beliefs are the key to really driving your actions and maintaining your goals, the 2logical system is hands down the best training I've ever taken.

What's impacted me the most from the 2logical training is the clarity that the course provides. It gives you real life examples of what you need to do as a manager and leader.

Once we started listening to our sales team and understanding what challenges they have and where there confidence levels and skill level were, we could really start helping them to address them and to make them stronger. We could make their weaknesses into strengths and give them that confidence that they require to get in front of customers and make sales and close deals. When we didn't talk on that level, and just drove actions, it really didn't do anything to help them progress or show them how to be better.

With the thoughts and beliefs, not only are you trying to make them better salespeople, but you coach them personally just as much as professionally. I think that makes all the difference in the world for how they receive the information and knowledge, knowing that you're trying to make them better.

We're hitting our deliverables faster and we probably have the most motivated sales team that's on the street right now.

I think the energy that this program drives; you can see it move through your organization. For our team specifically, once we started doing these things and setting the clear critical success factors and the goals and aligning all our systems necessary, I got feedback from people regarding our team, I got comments from competitors and everyone saying, "Man, when you see our people walking around town right now, you can just see that they're energized." We've even had ex-employees ask to come back and work with us again, just because that energy's been there. It's not just in the office, it's clearly when they leave here—they're proud to be part of this team and I think that's really what's driving us. Their desire to get better, the good feedback that they're getting from us now and helping them get there it's exciting, it's exciting to get that feedback from other guys.

After taking the 2logical course, I feel like I have an unfair advantage. I feel like I know things that other people should know. Other people should know this stuff, so I would 100% recommend 2logical to anybody who's interested in attaining their results and the goals of the organization, as well as developing their people; having a solid team beneath you. So if you want to be winners, man, 2logical's the way to go.

Life with Swagger

The energy business went through an extremely trying period, but Marc continued to persevere and succeed despite the adversities he faced. My friend and colleague, John Casey, received this subsequent letter from Marc about his team's successful results selling in turbulent times:

I was thinking of you over the last few days as I was reflecting on our year (prior to my year end review) and it has been a pretty challenging, yet fun ride over the past 12 months.

By implementing some of the leadership tactics that you taught me and the team, we have managed to gain market share and

the team's morale around the office has never been as good as it is now. And that is saying something given the pending merge, state of the industry and the fact that we just went through another round of layoffs.

Anyway, just wanted to say thanks again and we're going to continue to develop our leadership skills based on the 2logical training.

I hope our paths cross again soon.

All the best,

Marc

Brooke
Regional Mortgage Banking Firm

Numbers Tell a Story of Exponential Organizational Growth

Excerpt from video testimonial

From an executive position, what makes 2logical different from my perspective is it's training on the mindset and incorporating the whole person; not just our work world, but in fact our everyday real world, and the understanding that it's mindset that creates peak performance.

There's not a principle that I've been taught over my 20 year tenure with 2logical that I have not had the benefit of being able to apply in my personal world right along with my business world as well. I believe this is what truly sets 2logical apart in the marketplace and has had them have a definitive and transformative impact on people's lives.

2logical has helped us address our sales organization in a multitude of ways. Primarily from a mindset perspective and then cascading into skill-set and putting that to a business process to consistently be able to meet and exceed our goals.

Speaking in terms of results and working with 2logical, numbers tell a story, and we have been fortunate to exponentially grow the organization. We have circumstances where particular departments have doubled or more their sales results.

The first word that comes to mind when I think about 2logical is transformative. When I think about the impact on our organization from our relationship with 2logical and how they've helped us, it really comes in a couple of different levels. They've taught us about skill and process, but more importantly, it's been about a belief process; and helping not only myself, but our entire senior management team through to literally every individual who works for our organization. We believe so strongly in what it is 2logical brings to the table that we coordinate all of our staffing to be able to have 2logical training.

I'm not one to make recommendations easily but without question I can say that 2logical is the only organization that I would recommend regardless of industry, regardless of business type, regardless of where you are, whether you're at the peak or whether you're at the valley because with the training that they provide you can build from where you are, grow to be what you dream to be.

Life with Swagger

I have worked closely as an Executive Coach to Brooke for over 20 years. Through her timeless drive and commitment to help those she leads reach their full potential, we have helped countless numbers of people to live, love and sell their way to an extraordinary life fueled by swagger!

Todd
Top 5 Oil Services Company

The Manager that Set the Standard

When I went to your class last September I was not sure what I was going to do to change the attitude of the people of the yard that I had just been moved to manage. Once I got back to the office I went to work re-interviewing my people and getting a fill for their concerns and goals. After gathering all the information I put a plan together, first of all we came up with a mission statement and our goals. Then we ironed out the High Payoff Activities that would help us meet these goals.

One common theme that I heard from the guys was that they were tired of hearing how great another yard was and how they should just do things like they do. So I asked them as a group, "What have you done to change that?" They could not give me an answer, so I told them if you don't like something then change it, don't just complain about it. So this was how we got our Mission Statement of "Setting the Standard." I told them that if we perform to the best of our ability then we will make people say, "Look at how they do it, that is how things should be done." I have our HPAs posted in the main foyer of our office for our employees and customers to see.

We have since more than tripled our monthly revenue numbers and have done so without giving up our flawless execution. My area manager is also using our perfect inventory score as an example to other districts in our area. He told me that he is always telling our corporate leaders how great we are doing. I forwarded an e-mail that was sent from our Vice President to me and my boss saying that he hopes the other yards will be able to meet the bar that was set by us in future, to all of our team with the statement: "This is how we set the Standard."

My boss also told me that he has noticed a huge difference in the morale of the yard since I have been here. I am confident that without the instruction of Mr. Casey and the quotes that I get from you that I would have never been able to achieve the level of greatness that we have here. 2logical will continue to be very instrumental to my success as a manager in the future.

Life with Swagger

Todd followed up with this note:

I am very well. I hope that through my success that y'all can use my story to reach out to other struggling managers. What y'all do probably saves a lot of careers. I could not have imagined how well things are going over here. The guys are really excited about the future and I'm also starting to notice some of the ones who had stepped back are beginning to get more proactive and change their attitudes.

I know that we have some challenges ahead but I think that our future is very bright here. I am in the process of adding three more members of my team. Since we have added so much revenue I have been able to start updating the front offices and the shop to create a better work environment, enabling me to maintain the positive attitudes around here. They have also decided to expand us into the fishing tool product line which could have me triple in size in the next couple of years.

My supervisor and his boss were here the other day. Our Director was so impressed with my HPAs being posted in the main corridor that he took pictures; he was going to show the other managers and our VP. I sent an e-mail out to my team saying that now we have begun to not just set the standard in our area, but now we will set the standard across the nation, as our Director is over us and Southeast.

I hope that all is well with you and your family. My son that had the cleft pallet is doing great we are very blessed he is through with surgeries until he is 7 or 8. His pallet repair was smooth sailing and it healed perfectly. I feel that my newfound positive outlook has transferred over to my home life as well. My oldest started Kindergarten this year and so far he has been the model student. I really enjoy asking him what his favorite part of the day was. Again, I would like to thank you and your company for what y'all have done in my life. The lord is doing some amazing things through your business.

P.S. I remember you being an avid soccer player, what advice would you give my wife who is coaching 4 and 5 year old soccer kids? She wants to make sure they are learning and not just playing, but she wants to keep practice fun. Thanks.

Don
Top Tier Technology Company

The Tenured Rep Surprise

Excerpt from video testimonial

One of the things that I'm always concerned about in terms of bringing new training techniques or new training approaches to our organization is the fact that we have such a tenured sales force. The average tenure of our sales force is probably ten years.

There are a lot of training companies available to executives out there and I think 95% of them probably teach the same things the same way and 2logical takes a completely different approach that I think is relevant today, particularly for tenured reps and particularly for managers. I think the reason is, we all know in terms of the mechanics of selling, there aren't a lot of changes over the years, but in terms of, let's say the attitude with which you approach those mechanics and the things that you can learn as a tenured rep, 2logical's hitting the nail right on the head.

It's the group of tenured reps that are the hardest to reach and I think 2logical's approach reaches them better than anything I've seen before. Some of the comments I've received from my people were, some were fairly predictable and some were very surprising to me. The predictable comments that I received typically came from the newer reps, telling me how enthusiastically they were accepting the ideas that were being presented to them and that they were buying into it and that they liked it, and that it was a breath of fresh air.

The surprising comments to me were similar comments from our tenured reps and some of those were like, "This is the best training we've ever had," "I really appreciate the opportunity to be exposed to this kind of program," "I believe this is really going to change our organization, it's going to change me." I would definitely recommend 2logical to anyone who is trying to improve their sales organization.

Life with Swagger

As the National Sales Director, Don witnessed a plethora of sales training throughout his career, but none that had captured the hearts and minds of his people like 2logical's training. Under the strong leadership of my close friend and associate, Dave Naylor, the organization retained 2logical for over a decade perfecting the sales swagger of the organization. These efforts helped them gain market share and capture a leadership position across many product segments within industry.

Kevin
National Life Insurance Company

Mastering Fundamentals Shortens the Distance to the Top

Thanks for getting me involved in 2logical's sales training. Although it has only been a couple of days, my investment has already come back to me many fold.

Today, I began developing "Centers of Influence" for my business. This focused effort resulted in one of my favorite clients giving me ten quality referrals on the spot. In addition, we set up a meeting for next week to review a list of over one hundred local professionals that he knows personally.

Although I have achieved above average results since I entered the insurance industry, the majority of my business has come from methods of prospecting other than referrals. After attending your training program, I now realize I can and will be able to achieve my aggressive sales goals in a fraction of the time and with less effort.

I strongly recommend this course for any sales professional that has a sincere desire to enhance their sales results exponentially. The key to long-term sales success is working hard and smart. Thanks to your help, I can focus on doing both.

Best regards,

Kevin

Life with Swagger

When I first met Kevin, he was the most aggressive, persistent cold caller that I had ever met as a sales trainer...in my entire sales career. After helping Kevin realize that cold calling was the stepping stone to building a referral-based business, he went on to become a top producer within the insurance industry and a true leader.

A Force of One Hundred Thousand Souls
See more stories at 2logical.com/souls

Appendix B:

Recommended Resources

Appendix B

Recommended Resources

Timeless Books

- *Think and Grow Rich* by Napoleon Hill
- *As a Man Thinketh* by James Allen
- *As a Woman Thinketh* by Dorothy J. Hulst, James Allen
- *The Power of Positive Thinking* by Dr. Norman Vincent Peele
- *Psycho Cybernetics* by Maxwell Maltz
- *The Magic of Thinking* Big by David J. Swartz

2logical's Solutions & Resources

- 2logical's Legacy Sales Solution: Enterprise level sales solutions for regional, national and global sales forces. (www.2logical. com/landing/salesforcedevelopment.php - video summary)

- 2logical's Legacy Sales Leadership Solution: A masterful program used by countless Fortune 500 companies to transform Sales Leadership and Management performance. (www.2logical. com/landing/next-generation.php - video summary)

- 2logical's Sales Culture Development - Team, Division and Enterprise-Level Training Solutions.

- 2logical's world-renowned curriculum - Creating Results Capable™ Employees

- 2logical's World-Renowned Mindset Program - Self-Leadership: The Key to Professional and Personal Success;

  - Self-paced online course
    (www.2logical.com/self-leadership-course)

  - Classroom training
    (www.2logical.com/Self-Leadership-Sales-Course-Overview)

- 2logical's Train-the-Trainer Programs.
- Mi^6 - Motivational Intelligence™ Assessments, Solutions, Training Curriculums
- ⊗ **mojo**: Your private—professional and personal—coach for success; narrated by Joe Gianni (www.joinmojo.com).
- Momentum Meetings: Guided, video-based meetings to increase the focus, actions and success momentum of your team.

2logical's Sales Keynotes

- Selling in Turbulent Times
- Mindset: The Ultimate Sales Multiplier
- Selling with Swagger

2logical Video Testimonials

- Results (www.2logical.com/transforming_results_compilation)
- Transformation (www.2logical.com/transformational_compilation)
- Unique Training Approach (www.2logical.com/unique_training_approach)

Appendix C:

CAN SWAGGER BE IMPLEMENTED AT AN ENTERPRISE LEVEL?

Appendix C

CAN SWAGGER BE IMPLEMENTED AT AN ENTERPRISE LEVEL?

Can the power of Swagger be implemented on an enterprise level in major corporations?

Answer: Yes.

Can you give me an example?

Answer: Yes, countless examples!

Has the impact of Swagger Development been measured/documented?

Answer: Yes.

Can you give me an example?

Answer: Yes...Once again, I can share countless stories. However, perhaps the one that is most significant in my mind—and memorialized through an article published in Training Magazine—is the story of Oki Data Americas.

Example: Oki Data Americas Story

Time: Just prior to the 9/11 terrorist attack, the year of 2000.

The Challenge: The executives were redirecting the sales force with a new "go to market" strategy - transitioning from decades of strictly Channel Selling to the adoption of a Direct Selling Model.

Why the new change?

Answer: While extremely adept at selling dot matrix printers (maintaining a dominant market share), the resellers/dealers were largely ineffective at communicating Oki's color printer value proposition compared to other name brands and selling to the more sophisticated decision makers who made large color printing purchasing decisions.

What was the current state of the situation and level of results when 2logical first started?

Answer: Due diligence revealed that, while Oki Data enjoyed a dominant leadership position in the dot matrix printer market, the organization struggled to position and sell its new industry-leading color printers. Despite earning more than 20 major industry awards, corporate America remained largely unaware of their cutting-edge color LED printers.

Oki Data implemented sales skill training with their sales force to close the skill gaps needed for the transition. However, despite these efforts, it had not worked—and you and I know why. In fact, Oki Data's sales force had not made their sales plan for 36 consecutive months by applying skill training.

What solution was built and implemented?

Answer: 2logical implemented comprehensive sales management and sales force training that taught the "way of the sway." 2logical taught the entire company how to Swagger (training them extensively at the mindset level to leverage the sales skills/strategies needed for success).

What was the outcome?

Answer: The team began to hit its monthly sales goals consistently—for the first time in three years—following their indoctrination to Swagger.

Was this incredible impact/transformation measured/documented?

Answer: In 2003, the editors of Training Magazine were looking to publish an article to help its reader base rejuvenate their sales forces to counter the devastating negative effect the terrorist attacks of 9/11 had on commerce across most industries…

The editors of Training Magazine, taken aback by the uniqueness of 2logical's approach to sales talent development (leveraging skill and process training with mindset/belief—swagger-set training), asked to interview several clients. After interviewing the executives at Oki Data, they built a vignette into the article that featured the national sales manager, Vito Torregiano, memorializing the results of what happens when an entire sales force learns the "way of the sway."

Excerpt from Training Magazine

Torregiano selected 2logical to train his people after learning about the company's focus on developing the right "mindset" as well as sales skills. "It was the major difference [among the training companies]. The mindset piece really appealed to me and struck a chord with my managers," explained Torregiano.

2logical's mindset training addresses aspects ranging from being solution-oriented to maintaining a positive attitude and becoming self-motivated. It starts with getting salespeople to be 100 percent responsible for themselves. "If you can't get people to do that, any other training you do with them is destined to fail," says David Naylor, EVP of 2logical.

Some 65 salespeople went through 56 hours of sales training in groups of 15-25. Those same sales- people then went out and increased color printer sales by nearly 200 percent. "We grew our pipeline by about 300 percent as well. It was a function of getting in front of the customer," Torregiano says. "When you look at the end result, I have a very confident sales force now."

Appendix D:

ACKNOWLEDGMENTS

Appendix D

Acknowledgments

Adrienne Dake
Al Picchi
Al West
Amy Paone
Angela Durkin
Ann Conroy
Anna Schlata
Ben Trewin
Benjamin Laura
Benjamin Naylor
Beth Schumacher
Betsy White
Bill Manza
Bill McDonnell, Jr.
Bill Thomas
Bob Doran
Boomer Esiason
Brad Groff
Brian Francis
Brooke Anderson-Tompkins
Buddy Howell
Carlos Garzon
Carly Hochreiter
Carole Montpare
Catherine Naylor
Chad Rains
Charleen Allen
Charlet Riddell
Charlie Newton
Chris Riegle
Chuck Wheeler
Cindy Capodagli

Colleen Smolarek
Craig LaDuke
Craig Mueller
Cynthia LuBecke
Dan Drees
Dan Watson
Daniel Porter
Daniele Bovenzi
Darlene Krawczyk
Dave Bilyeu
David Donnovan
David Naylor
Dawn Stevens
Dennis Walker
Derek Allan
Dion Vlachos
Don Roesch
Don Snowden
Doug Hayes
Ed Hartzell
Edward, Eddie, Yankus
Ellen Nichols
Eric D Munden
Frank Buono
Frank Viola
Fred Collins
Gary Johansen
Gene O'Donovan
Gene Rattermen
Glen Rothe
Glenn Gordon
Gonzalez, Plinio J

Graeme H. Falconer
Graham Carson
Gregg Eddinger
Helayne Klier
Howard Warner
Iain McIntosh
Ivy J. Oubre
Jackson Casey
James Dwyer
James Nowicki
Jason Close
Jean Bradley
Jeanne Heinrich
Jeanne Olson
Jeff Briggs
Jeff Fanselow
Jen Senich
Jeremy Lofts
Jim Giblin
Jim Green
Joan Malay
Joe Cheatham
Joe Grube
Joe Williams
John Baughman
John Billington
John Casey
John Colaruotolo
John Fortunato
John Guzzo
John Hill
John Kist
John M Thompson
John Reilly
John W Austin
Jon Yaeger
Jordan Gianni
Joseph, Jo-Jo, Kennedy
Judy Stewart

Karl Bullard
Kathleen Fisher
Kathy Shirley
Kelley Taylor
Ken Marshall
Ken Wojnowski
Kent Clapp
Kevin Crawford
Kevin Sheehan
Knut Henriksen
Kris Murphy
Kristen Nablo
Larry Levenberg
Laura Casey
Lee Gleason
Len Clementi
Lloyd, Bubba, Boudreaux
M Abdullah Al-Ammari
Macel Pontbriand
Marc Carriere
Marc Hebner
Marcus Haor
Margarita Gorokhovsky
Maria Claudia Borras
Maria Moffa
Marilyn Mitchell
Mark Bradford
Mark Brown
Mark Claus
Mark Colosi
Mark Guinn
Mark Huber
Mark Re
Matthew Whitehead
Merle Whitehead
Michael Fossaceca
Michael Hoffman
Michael J Sparacino
Michelle Gianni

Michelle Naylor
Michelle Schultz
Mike Coluzzi
Mike Johnson
Morgan Gianni
Mr. "E"
Nannette Nocon
Nathan Hickman
Neil A McBride
Nicole Sherrill
Nikki Upshaw
Noah Gianni
Pamela Booker
Patrick Casey
Paul Madero
Peter Novak
Randi Minetor
Randy Farnsworth
Randy Hall
Ray A Watson
Rayed B Al-Eskandrani
Richard Johnson
Rob Gilbert
Robert, Randy, Nemec
Rod Larson
Ronnie MacGregor
Russell & Xandra Turner
Ryan Stephens
Samantha Cline
Sandy Morgart
Scott Klenk
Scott Souter
Scott Welch
Sean Johnson
Sharon Gillespie
Steve Christopherson
Steve D'Eredita
Steve Gaglio
Steve Harling

Steve Kahn
Steve McDonnell
Steve McDonnell, Jr.
Sue LaVallee
Terry McHugh
Thad DeMulder
Tiffany S Pitts
Todd Harper
Tom Jones
Tom Russell
Tony Smith
Tony Tortorella
Troy Keeping
Vince Lambardo
Vito Torregiano
W Clement Stone
Wayne Symons
Wes Bryne
Wes Culler
Will McDonnell
William Tepe
Zach Caravetta
Zvonimir Djerfi

CPSIA information can be obtained
at www.ICGtesting.com
Printed in the USA
BVOW04*1052030317
477707BV00006B/17/P